Adventures
in
Wood
Finishing

88 Rue de Charonne

Adventures in Wood Finishing

George Frank

The Taunton Press

Editor: *Laura Cehanowicz Tringali*
Designer: *Roger Barnes*
Layout and illustrations: *Christopher Clapp*
Editorial assistant: *Marianne Seidler*
Production coordinator: *Cindy Lee*
Typesetting: *Nancy-Lou Knapp*
Pasteup: *Kathy Olsen, Jean Zalkind*

Typeface: Compugraphic Goudy Oldstyle, 11 pt. text
Paper: Warren Olde Style, Wove Offset, 70 lb.
Printer and binder: R. R. Donnelley & Sons Co., Chicago, Ill.

The Taunton Press, Inc.
52 Church Hill Road
Box 355
Newtown, Connecticut 06470

Printed in the United States of America

Contents

Preface

Out of wood one can turn a salad bowl, bend a rocking chair, carve a statue, construct a house and craft furniture and violins, but, regardless of the millions of forms wrought wood may take, it must always be finished. The number of books written on woodturning, furniture making and all the rest of the woodworking trades is endless. Libraries are filled with them. On wood finishing, however, perhaps a dozen books are printed, all reiterating the same old facts and formulas. I have tried not to repeat what can so easily be found elsewhere.

I have spent my life learning, inventing and improvising ways and means of finishing wood, and the trade has compensated me well. In 1924 in Paris, we wood finishers had a table set just for us in a local restaurant, because no decent people wanted to sit near our dirty bunch. Fifteen years later, an ex-prince asked me to honor his table with my presence. This book is about the stopovers on the road between those two tables—about what I learned, my experiments, trials and errors, successes and failures. Because most wood-finishing problems are as individual as the craftsmen dealing with them, I have also included sections containing specific problems selected from the Questions & Answers column of Fine Woodworking magazine, for which I am a consulting editor.

In this book I speak as a friend, not as a scholar. I would be the last to think that I have the final word on any subject. Wood finishing is a young, growing art, and all that I know about it is in this book. Much, much more remains to be said and done. I hope I will succeed in encouraging someone to say it, do it.

—George Frank
South Venice, Fla., 1980

Introduction

France was among the winners of World War I; my country, Hungary, was among the losers. A few years after the signing of the Treaty of Trianon, which took away more than half of Hungary's land, there was total economic collapse. Even with my brand-new work permit (testifying that I had completed my apprenticeship and was a full-fledged cabinetmaker) plus a diploma (earned in evening school) dubbing me master of stains and wood coloring, I spent more days sitting on the benches of placement offices than working. The last job I had held, in a suburb of Budapest, was in a pigsty. Pigs and shop were under the same roof, a divider of less than six feet high separating us.

So I begged and borrowed (mostly from my poor mother) the fare to Paris, and arrived there on the first day of May 1924. The only person I knew in the city, a carpenter at the Renault automobile factory, assured me that if I went with him I would be able to start work as a carpenter right away. So the next morning we traveled to the factory, which was just outside of Paris. At 8:00 A.M. the hiring began for the four carpenter positions that were available and by 9:00 A.M. it was all over, the positions filled by more aggressive applicants who spoke the language. I had no idea where to go next; I didn't know how to use the subway, nor could I afford a subway ride.

The Eiffel Tower is such a landmark that regardless of where you are you can see it—I decided it must be somewhere near the center of the city and began walking toward it. The six-mile walk took me through a section of Paris where there wasn't a single woodworking shop, but to my relief, when I arrived at the tower, I found the area teeming with activity. Dozens of carpenters were hammering, sawing and nailing, erecting shacks and booths for a coming fair. I walked straight into the *Bureau d'Embauche* and was hired, after negotiating in sign language and with the help of a pocket dictionary, as a painter. Then my new employer took me to the door and quizzically pointed his finger to the top of the tower. I nodded my head quickly, without hesitation, and he made me understand I was to go eat lunch and return in an hour.

For lunch I munched on a single roll, then joined a group of about ten men at the base of the tower, each bundled up in three or four shirts and double dungarees. A series of elevator rides took us to the top of the tower. The last elevator car was our workroom, loaded with all the paraphernalia of painting, and it stopped about thirty feet under the last platform of the tower. A door in the roof of the cab was opened, and we climbed through, one by one. A broad safety belt was attached to each of us; a brush with an eight-foot handle was thrust into my hands. The foreman showed me a huge beam to paint, and I had the shock of my life. The beam was at least five feet away from me, and not only did I have nothing to lean on or to grab hold of, to my great horror we were moving. The whole tower was swaying as it still sways today, slowly but constantly, a few feet to and fro. Although this swaying did not agree with me at all, I clenched my teeth and painted until a new enemy, the wind, lifted its ugly head. Unlike my companions, I was dressed lightly, and the May wind froze my hands on the brush. My eyes and nose were running, and my head was swaying with the tower. Then the brush fell out of my hands, the world blacked out and peace descended at last.

When I opened my eyes I was sitting on a bench in the park and an elderly matron, an attendant at the tower's first-aid station, was waking me up with smelling salts. Later on she told me that her husband was a carpenter and that in Paris the woodworking trade was concentrated in one area, the Faubourg Saint Antoine, not far from where I lived. She handed me two francs and fifty centimes, money my employer had given her to give to me for my small part in refinishing the Eiffel Tower—the first money I earned in France. By 3:30 P.M. I was in the woodworker's section of Paris, and by 4:30 P.M. I was hired as a wood finisher, to start working the next morning. This was the period when skilled workers were badly needed in Paris. It was a worker's market.

As a painter of steel towers I did not turn out to be the best, but as a wood finisher I have always held my own. My first employer in the trade manufactured "antiques," and although I did not like him or his work ethic, I held onto the job for three long weeks. I worked sixty to seventy hours each week, lived in a cheap hotel and saved every centime. On my third payday I paid back—with interest—the money I had borrowed from mother.

My second job, with another furniture manufacturer, found me the only male employee among fifteen female ones. This job also lasted three weeks; I was fired—the only job from which I was fired ever—for kissing one of my workmates during working hours. That evening, however, the boss who had fired me offered me a better job in his factory out of town. I was more independent by then though, less scared, and didn't take it.

My next boss was Ferdinand Schnitzspan, a man with a heart of gold. Here at last my salary and working conditions reached the standards of 1924-25. Over two hundred men worked in this large architectural woodworking plant, which housed under its roof all the woodworking trades. In this hierarchy, the woodcarvers were the princes. They wore spotless *blouses blanches* (white smocks) and considered themselves artists. Closely following them in importance were the gilders, also garbed in white smocks. The proletariat of this world were the wood finishers. Compared to central European standards we fared well, but compared to the other wood trades in Paris we lagged far behind. We dressed any way we pleased, and usually a dirty apron camouflaged our secondhand attire. Our hands were never clean (no rubber gloves for us yet) and some of us did not smell pleasant. We ate apart from other diners in the local restaurant, where a table was set especially for our group. The most frequent topic of conversation was wood finishing, and we often spoke of a shop in Paris where wood finishers wore the princely *blouses blanches*.

This haven was the Maison Jansen, and I made up my mind to work there. At the time it was one of the best interior decorating establishments in the world. Kings, emperors, kaisers and dictators would rather abdicate than have their palaces decorated by anyone else, and leaders from the five continents begged for Jansen's services. Jansen's showrooms were and still are at the very heart of Paris, on the Rue Royale; their factory, as large as a city block and five stories high, was at the Rue Saint Sabin. On the second floor of this factory was the finishing atelier, presided over by Fernand Naveilhan, a man who ruled with absolute authority. He never hired a worker with less than fifteen years' experience, but while he was strict, he treated his workers well. In turn, they respected him for his knowledge and for

George Frank at his villa, in 1927. In this garden the fifteen samples, which won for Frank the coveted job at Jansen, were created.

his unending search for perfection. Like many of his countrymen at the time, Naveilhan was a rabid chauvinist. The foreign-born had little chance of getting a job in his shop. This knowledge only intensified my resolution.

In the meantime, my standing with Schnitzspan improved. I became one of his best workers and reaped the reward for it. Whenever we had work out of town—with generous extra pay—I was a member of the team, and more than once in full charge of it. For two years I worked for this huge man and took a great liking to him, and he reciprocated in his own grumbling way. Then, I do not know why, he lost his best customer, and our ways parted. Schnitzspan's loss was Casetta's gain. This wood-finishing outfit, one of the biggest in Paris, received the rich contract, and since I was well versed in its technicalities I was hired without further ado. Here, too, I made fast progress and again became a permanent member of the best-paid traveling team. My lifestyle changed with this new affluence. Secondhand clothing was no longer for me; my suits were custom-made by tailors. I ate in better restaurants and while for years I had lived decently in the Latin Quarter of Paris, I now moved into an elegant villa in the suburbs. Still there was one thing I wanted—the job at Jansen.

During my leisure time I experimented with new and unusual finishes, such as filling the pores of wood decoratively (upon which I will elaborate later), and made samples of my work. I made two sets of fifteen samples each and, when finished, took one set to Agisson, my boss at Casetta's. He had never seen finishes like mine, and I laid down my terms: a fair amount of cash, a two-year contract as foreman in the shop and an increase in pay. "Let me keep your samples for a few days and I will let you know my answer," Agisson said.

Patience is not one of my virtues. For two weeks Agisson did not make a move. So I freshened up my second set of samples and, one weekday morning, presented them to the three greatest furniture dealers in Paris: Mercier Frères, Kriéger and Au Bûcheron. They made a great impression everywhere. Questions were asked, possibilities debated and excellent jobs offered, but I was not interested. These three were mere practice for the real interview—with Jansen.

Early that afternoon I handed my resignation to Agisson. *I had gotten a foreman's job at Jansen.* Without a word he handed me my samples and left the room. He knew Jansen—everybody knew Jansen.

This was the last day of April 1928. Four years earlier I had boarded the Paris-bound train in Budapest, where I had worked in a pigsty.

Two days later I met Fernand Naveilhan. He was short, stocky, sharp, witty, cunning and ready to fight. He knew all about me, while I knew little about him. Naveilhan knew, for instance, that I had been hired for two reasons, first, because I was a wizard with colors, and second, because of his excessive drinking. I was to replace him if he failed, though I knew nothing of this at the time.

In spite of this, Naveilhan greeted me without a trace of hostility or jealousy. We talked shop for hours, and before we knew it, it was noon, and Naveilhan asked me to be his guest for lunch. By then we knew we were friends, two of a kind, with similar plans and ambitions. We went together in his chauffeur-driven car to a cozy place frequented by connoisseurs of good cheer.

Upon returning to the factory after lunch, Naveilhan took me on a guided tour of the wood-finishing shop. It was fifty years ahead of its time—clean, spacious, orderly and organized. Near every bench was a sink with hot and cold water, outlets for electricity, compressed air and vacuum. There were rooms with heat lamps, others with live steam and still others reserved for removing old finishes and paints. The thirty to forty men working there were the best the trade could offer and wore the *blouses blanches*, protected by a plastic apron. They worked without pressure, with a single purpose: to produce the best possible work and to earn a nod of satisfaction from Naveilhan. In this shop the performers of the trade became respected professionals, acting with well-deserved dignity and pride.

The tour over, Naveilhan told me that he would gladly relinquish all this to me if I would promise to continue what he had started, to keep the shop and its spirit up, and to allow him to sweep the floors as long as he was able. The greatest compliment I ever had in my long life was when this man approved me as his successor. Although I told him I had no intention of replacing him—even if I could—I promised him that to the best of my ability I would continue his work and help wood finishing grow into a skill, a science and an art. In this book I have tried to keep that promise.

Protection

Chapter One

There are only two reasons for finishing wood: to protect it and to embellish it. In this chapter I will talk about protection.

The use of wood is not reserved for the fine woodworker alone. Whether one makes flooring, gutters, houseboats, iceboxes or joists, the problem remains how to protect the wood from termites, worms, marine borers, fungi and bacteria. All these are ready and willing to weaken or destroy the wood, or at least to shorten its useful life.

Man's genius did not stay idle in the face of these dangers, and modern technology has found effective ways to deal with most of them. Pressure-treated lumber, for instance, is a godsend to the woodworking industry. Huge kilns evaporate most of the water in the wood, and the empty cells are filled under pressure with a watery solution of mineral salts. The water is again evaporated, leaving a residue of salts within the wood that renders the wood useless as food for insects and fungi or fuel for fire. In more and more areas, laws and regulations mandate the use of treated lumber in home building. Simple horse sense dictates its use where wood is exposed to moisture, mildew, rot or insects. Abundant and authoritative information is available at a moderate cost from the American Wood Preservers' Institute, 1651 Old Meadow Rd., McLean, Va. 22102.

While the use of treated lumber is vitally important in many woodworking trades, for the fine woodworker the interest is limited. One reason is that about ninety-five percent of treated lumber is softwood, inappropriate for refined projects. But here is a surprise. Broadly speaking, wood is treated with one of three solutions: with creosote or coal-tar solution; with oil-borne solutions such as pentachlorophenol, copper-8-quinolinolate or tributyl-tin-oxide; or with water-borne solutions such as acid copper chromate, ammoniacal copper arsenate, chromated copper arsenate or chromated zinc chloride.

Lumber that has been pressure-treated with water-borne chemicals emerges from the vat with accentuated markings, the latewood greatly emphasized. Frank crafted this small coffee table from scraps of pressure-treated 2x4s, 2x6s and 2x8s, bartered from local carpenters with a six-pack of beer.

This last category is the least expensive, most popular of the three, and it holds special interest for fine woodworkers. Water-borne chemicals injected into the wood darken the hard areas while hardly affecting the soft ones, thereby emphasizing the natural markings of the wood. Pine, spruce and hemlock are the most frequently treated woods, and all of these come out of the vat more beautiful than when put in, their markings far more pronounced.

Here is an example of how to take advantage of this. I have been married to the same lady for the past forty-nine years—such a record can hardly be achieved without divergences of opinion here and there. The most recent one concerned new kitchen flooring. I prefer soft carpeting, easy to walk on and to keep clean, while Catherine prefers vinyl or tile, which can be mopped clean and will "last forever" and look good.

Neither of those preferences won out. Why? Because I remembered that after the world's first subway line was completed in Hungary in 1896, the most elegant avenue in Budapest, under which this new marvel ran, had to be resurfaced. This was done with wood blocks the size of bricks. The blocks were soaked in thinned-down tar to protect them from fungi, termites, rot and water, then laid end grain up on top of a smooth concrete base that was covered with tar. There were no automobiles in 1896, but a Rolls Royce cannot match the elegance of a Hungarian nobleman driving the four matched horses of his carriage; the sound of the feet of the felt-shod horses striking the wooden pavement has no modern-day equivalent. (Unfortunately, this street covering was destroyed around 1919, the wood blocks stolen by the people and used for fuel.)

By now you must have guessed it: We are toying with the idea of installing a modernized version of this road covering in our kitchen and I have already carried out the first experiment. About a hundred yards from my house a new one is being built. A few good words and a six-pack of beer helped me to make friends with the carpenters, who then allowed me to pick up all the short scraps of pressure-treated lumber (mostly 2x4s, 2x6s and 2x8s) on the site. I crosscut these scraps to about ⅜ inch long on my table saw and glued them with white glue onto a piece of two-foot-square particle board for the top of a small coffee table. The job, properly sanded and finished with three coats of polyurethane, certainly does not look like scrap wood, as you can see from the photos on the previous page. My tabletop and my proposed kitchen floor are but two examples of how wood, embellished by protective treatment, can be put to good use.

Protection from Fire

Insects and fungi, although powerful, are not the sole enemies of wood. The most feared one is fire. Thus the wood-preserving industry came up with a seemingly perfect solution, and now wood can be treated to be fire-retardant, too. This is a mixed blessing. The obvious advantage is that the treated wood will not burn. Consequently in case of fire it may save lives. On the other hand, although fire-retardant wood does not burn, if subjected to intense heat it produces smoke, and smoke can kill as well as fire. Another plus is that fire-retardant lumber creates jobs—at the treating plants, in the shops (where special carbide-tipped tools are needed to work with such lumber) and in the administration, where complicated and bewildering regulations are made, published and enforced. The dust produced by the saw, the shaper and all the other machines while working with such wood is, however, noxious. I have worked with fire-retardant wood and I am convinced that its dust causes more harm than the protection such wood offers from fire is worth. The poor worker spitting his lungs out dies less spectacularly than one killed by fire, but dies just the same. The hazards caused by the dust of fire-retardant wood should be thoroughly investigated.

Availability, or lack of it, is another disadvantage of fire-retardant wood. While the American Wood Preservers' Institute states that pressure-treated wood that is highly fire-retardant is readily available, this is simply not so. It's hard to find treated choice hardwoods suitable for fine woodworking, and even if you're lucky enough to find a supply, the treated hardwood will never match the treated plywood of the same species. This is simply because only the core stock of the plywood, not the face, is fire-retardant.

Let's not forget the bewildering rules and regulations pertaining to fire-retardant wood. In the late 1960s, I went to see one of the high officials at New York City Hall, with a booklet containing these regulations in hand. I politely asked for an explanation of the regulations, only to be told that nobody on the premises understood them either.

Facing these difficulties and many unreasonable demands in the 1960s, many otherwise honest woodworkers of my acquaintance were forced to choose questionable ways out. Some inspectors could be bribed, and sometimes the wood that was sent to the laboratory to be tested and approved was not the same wood we used on the job. The next story will illustrate my point.

The flimflammed fire inspector—The Washington Irving House is an elegant building that sits on the corner of 16th Street and 3rd Avenue in New York City. In the early 1960s, I was contracted to line the lobby walls with dark walnut paneling. I was an old hand at the game, and I knew well that on this job every piece of wood had to be fire-retardant.

I measured the job carefully and figured that 990 square feet of paneling would be needed. If I ordered thirty-one 4x8 panels, I would have only two square feet left over. Four or five weeks later, thirty-one flitch-matched walnut panels were installed in the lobby, all stamped, approved and certified as fire-retardant in compliance with city regulations.

On the last day of the job, the architect noticed an area on the wall where a fuse box had been removed, exposing an unfinished spot about two square feet—the size of my leftover panel. How seldom it happens, thought I, that one can use up the last square inch of lumber on a job. I gave instructions to Joe, my man in charge, to do the work. Two minutes later Joe reported that the panel was two inches too short, so I called up the shop and told my foreman to make up a panel. In a short while Joe had the new panel—not treated, not stamped, not certified—when, lo and behold, the fire inspector arrived. He had so much gold on his uniform that we knew he was somebody important. He snatched the panel from Joe's hand, looked it over and declared, "This is not fire-retardant. Where is your boss?" I appeared, and the inspector repeated his charge. I dug in my briefcase and came up with the invoice from the Georgia-Pacific Company for the thirty-one fire-retardant panels. "I don't give a hoot about your thirty-one panels," bellowed the inspector. "You may have installed them on another job. All I know is that I caught you red-handed, and if you know what's good for you, you'll take down all the panels by tomorrow so I can inspect them one by one."

He handed back the small panel and I did some fast thinking. "Inspector," said I, "if I proved that this panel does not burn, would you be satisfied?" "Yes, I would be," he said, "but I know the difference between treated and untreated wood."

I struck a match to a sheet of newspaper, waited until it was burning well, and then held the panel over it. The paper burned itself out and I had to drop it. The panel smoked, but did not catch fire. With that, the inspector scribbled on his form and handed it to me. The job had passed inspection; the inspector left. Now it was Joe's turn to shake his head. "Boss," he asked me, "you know the panel isn't fire-retardant, so why didn't it burn?" "Joe, my boy," said I, "if you had watched me closely, you would know the reason. A flame is much cooler where it originates, and by holding the panel so close to the paper, I exposed it to far less heat than it needed to catch fire. Plus, I moved the fire so that no one area was exposed too long to the heat."

This is a true story—990 square feet of paneling in that lobby are genuinely fire-retardant; under three square feet are not, but they did not burn. I hope that if the inspector is still alive, he will bear no grudge against me.

Fungi and insects will attack untreated wood if it is exposed to them, fire never will. Fire is always caused by carelessness. It is not the wood that should be made fire-retardant; people should be taught to be more careful.

Protection from Moisture

Protection is the topic of this chapter and so far I have talked about protection from living organisms and from fire. Now I will discuss protection from moisture.

Regardless of age, wood will always absorb moisture from the air and from contact with water or moist objects. It will release moisture when exposed to dry air, heat or wind. Absorbed moisture will cause the wood to be heavier and its width to expand; loss of moisture will cause it to be lighter and its width to shrink.

A few years back, a New York college purchased four heavy wooden tables for use in its greenhouse. Within a few months the tops of all four warped quite badly. Examination disclosed that the plants stored on the tables were watered frequently and that the tabletops were almost constantly wet. In addition, the undersides were exposed to heating elements installed under the tables. Of course, the upper sides of the tables expanded and the undersides shrank—all four tabletops assumed a graceful, but highly impractical, convex shape.

To remedy this, I suggested a simple four-point program: 1) Temporarily reverse the tabletops; 2) when the former upper sides (now undersides) have dried out and regained their original shape, coat both sides and all edges with at least three coats of marine varnish; 3) install two layers of insulating material between the heaters and the undersides of the tables; 4) place metal pans on the tabletops to catch the water from the plants. All this was done, and the tabletops are straight and the college is satisfied.

The wood finisher's concern, however, is not so much the correction of warping or twisting caused by an imbalance of moisture as it is the prevention of moisture absorption or loss. Experiments have proved that wood brought to about ten percent moisture content will shrink and expand less under normal living conditions. Controlled kiln-drying of lumber is therefore a great deterrent to warping caused by moisture imbalance. So is the use of inert materials, such as particle board or pressed board, as core stock in plywood.

All finishes protect against moisture to a certain extent. A heavy coating of wax will keep water out of wood for a few hours. Shellac will resist longer, varnish longer yet, special marine varnishes may protect the wood for years.

I am frequently asked for a good finish for outdoor furniture, usually made of redwood. Many hardware stores advise using redwood stains, but often these turn out to be mostly paint and flake off eventually. Here is what I recommend:

After sanding the furniture down to the bare wood, mix two-thirds of boiled linseed oil and one-third of any good brand of marine varnish. Spread this mixture generously on the furniture, but before it dries—about fifteen minutes to a half hour later—wipe off all that you possibly can. Use a burlap-type rag, and plenty of elbow grease. The very thin coating that remains in the wood will offer surprisingly good protection, but it can still be improved by repetition. Give each application a week to dry and put the emphasis on the rubbing. That is what will make it beautiful.

Regardless of the type of wood you're working with and the finish you select, remember to finish all surfaces of the work evenly. Forget or neglect to do this and you will likely end up with cupped boards. In my shop both sides of doors are finished with the same finish, and wood paneling has a cheaper, but balancing finish applied to the back. In addition to preventing moisture from the walls from penetrating the paneling, this is a good way to use up leftover finish from other jobs. For instance, most wood finishers, when they need four gallons of a colored lacquer, will buy or mix at least five gallons and have a gallon or so extra. Just be sure that you use the same type of material on the back of the paneling as you do on the front.

Changing the Color of the Wood

Chapter Two

Imagine that your next project is to build a simple coffee table. First you will decide its shape and size and draw the plans. Next you will select and secure the wood. The protection of wood and its embellishment, the true goals of the wood finisher, go hand in hand. While still at the planning stage your next concern will be how to protect your table from spilled water or liquor, cigarette burns, scratches, nicks and inkspots. You may also wonder how to make your rough wood better looking and more elegant.

Regardless of whether you opt for an easily available native wood such as pine, oak or maple, or for an imported variety such as rosewood, zebrawood or bubinga, you have only three ways to make the wood more beautiful: You can change its color, you can change its tactile quality (make it smoother or rougher) or you can highlight its natural markings.

When a lady changes the color of her hair and the lovely chestnut crown becomes platinum overnight, the reason for this change is a belief that the new color improves her appearance. No man in his right senses would ever dare to contest that this is so, but the truth is that dyeing often obliterates the many subtle variations of natural hair color and makes the hair monochromatic.

The same holds true for wood. Changing its color will always make it different, but not necessarily more beautiful. Just like hair, wood never has a solid, even color. The pine you considered for your coffee table ranges in color from white to light brown. Maple ranges from milky white to grayish yellow. Oak has the full scale of straw and wheat. Carefully and skillfully applied coloring may not only preserve the original variations of the wood but may even underscore them, while careless coloring may silence forever the symphony of natural colors. Therefore, regardless of whether you are making your project of pine, maple or oak, don't color it unless a series of samples convinces you that the new color is really more pleasant than the natural one. Don't change the color of the wood unless you have to.

But before proceeding to a discussion of ways to change the color of the wood, let me digress in order to discuss that very important but oft-neglected aspect of wood finishing, lighting in the workshop.

Finishing-Shop Lighting

More wood is ruined by finishing under improper lighting than it is by any other single cause. Yet not many craftsmen worry about the light in their finishing rooms, and I've never seen any guidelines in books. So here is my own opinion on the subject.

You must have as much light as possible and it must be as close as possible to natural daylight. Six-foot or eight-foot long fluorescent fixtures, with half the tubes cool white and half daylight-imitating, are your best bet. Install them as high as possible, well sheltered from dust, and clean them frequently.

Don't install the lights directly over the working area. The object you are working on should reflect the light to your eyes. If you were to replace the object you are working on with a mirror, you should be able to see in it the whole light fixture. The lower the angle of reflection the better, the ideal being about forty-five degrees. This means that the angle between your eyes, the work and the light should be about ninety degrees. I would go a step further and install one or two movable lights about six feet off the floor, so you can arrange the light to reflect off the top of a high piece like a chair or chest.

Lights near the work or over the spraying area will have to be inside protective fixtures, and you might have to use incandescents. But remember that all artificial lights distort colors—incandescents, for example, add a definite red hue. Never match colors by artificial light. Do it by daylight and in shadow.

Here's a trick I've often used in my shop to match a color perfectly. Take a piece of clean white paper that measures about two inches by four inches and fold it down the center. Now you have a double sheet measuring two inches by two inches. Punch a ¼-inch to ½-inch hole

Color to match   **Matching color**

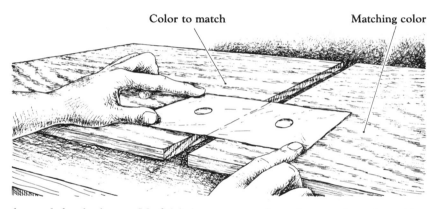

through both sheets. Unfold the paper and put it over the color to be matched and a sample of the color that you think matches it. Looking through the holes and comparing the two will allow you to detect even the slightest difference in color.

Stains, Dyes and Pigments

We all love wood because of its endless variety of grain. To put the natural markings of the wood in evidence is the true task of anyone who tries to beautify it through finishing.

To me, the first requisite of a beautiful finish is that it must remain readable. This means that the grain or the markings of the wood must remain clearly visible after the finish is applied. It also means that from the grain of the wood, trained people should be able to read

Weak solutions of various chemicals can greatly accentuate the natural markings of the wood. For example, potassium dichromate gives the illusion of great depth to mahogany, left, while ferrous sulfate brings out the contrasting figure in 'palazota' maple, right.

the whole history of the tree—its origin, age and environment; its fights for survival; its adventures.

Wood finishing is the stepchild of the woodworking industry. Even its vocabulary is misleading. We use the word staining when we refer to a chemical action that changes the color of the wood, to a process where a dye brings this change about, or to a process where we cover the wood with a colored film or a thin layer of colored pigment. Only this last method should rightly be called staining. The first two should be called dyeing. The difference between dyeing and staining is like the difference between getting a deep suntan and using makeup to imitate one. Dyes and dyeing will not affect the readability of the wood, in fact, at times dye will even help to emphasize the wood's natural markings. Stains and staining, on the other hand, will always reduce the readability. However, stains do have great merit, especially on the production line. Ease of application is one, but far more important is staining's help in achieving uniform coloring. This, especially on the assembly line, is a fair compensation for reduced readability.

Chemicals—Cuban mahogany is the color of raw steak. Sponge it with a solution of potassium dichromate and its color deepens considerably. Not only does it become a dark rusty red, but the contrast between the light and dark markings is accentuated. This chemical process, wrongly called staining, enhances the beauty of the wood. Napoleon's craftsmen often used this process, and most French Empire furniture is "stained" by this method.

It is a well-known fact that wheat-colored oak becomes brownish-gray when sponged with ammonia. Here is a short story about another chemical action. In 1938, a Pennsylvania manufacturer imported a shipload of timber from Europe. To mystify the competition, he gave it the name palazota. It looked like bird's-eye maple, but was whiter and had more eyes. He made bedroom suites of it and sold them successfully. By 1942 the market was saturated with white palazota bedrooms, and dealers were asking for something new. Since the manufacturer had over two-thirds of his lumber still in stock, he tried stains, but the stains obliterated most of the delicate markings of the wood and the stained palazota did not sell. That is when I was called in. After three weeks of experimenting, I found the answer: A weak solution of ferrous sulfate brought unbelievable changes to the wood.

The miniature eyes opened up considerably, while the flat areas remained almost unchanged. The wood seemed to acquire a third dimension—depth. When I added some coloring dye to the ferrous chemical, I produced a whole new array of decorative effects. Regardless of whether the palazota was tinted gray, brown, gold or red, its markings sang out loud and clear. Three years later, the manufacturer did not have a single board left in his factory.

A simple experiment illustrates the possibilities: Apply potassium dichromate solution to pieces of birch and maple, and the wood becomes pleasantly dyed a rich yellow color. Apply the solution to a piece of oak, and the wood becomes a dark rusty brown. So far so good. Now, imagine that somehow you can get a cake of logwood extract (also called extract of campeche wood). Dissolve one ounce in a pint of water, and with this winelike brew sponge the three pieces of wood with which you are experimenting. Let dry, sandpaper lightly and apply another coat of potassium dichromate solution. After an hour you will find that the birch and the maple have become rusty brown, and the oak a rich chocolate color.

If you plan to experiment with potassium dichromate, here is a basic formula to get you started. Dissolve about $1\frac{3}{4}$ ounces of potassium dichromate crystals in a pint of (preferably) rainwater. Keep this concentrated solution in a bottle, and experiment on scrap wood with more diluted solutions. To start, take another pint of water and add to it two-tenths of your concentrated dichromate. Saturate the wood. Take up any excess liquid with a well-squeezed sponge and let the wood dry thoroughly, for half a day at least. Then check to see how far you are from your goal. Generally, chemical dyes should be used in weaker concentrations than aniline dyes and applied repeatedly. This is because they show their final effect only after thorough drying. (Remember, it is far more difficult to lighten the wood than to darken it.)

Dissolving one ounce of potassium permanganate in a pint of water produces a dye that will turn most hardwoods a pleasant brown. The tint, however, will fade and change color from brown-violet to brown. If the color you get is too dark, wash down the wood with a fairly strong solution of sodium thiosulfate (available from photo-supply stores as hypo solution). You will get a nicely bleached wood.

Another coloring chemical can be prepared by mixing equal

amounts of ordinary vinegar and water, then throwing in all the rusty iron you can find—old nails, screws, hinges and tools. Let the solution sit for a week, then filter it through a piece of cloth. The resulting liquid will produce a silvery gray color on oak. It won't be so effective, though, on woods lacking tannic acid. This can be remedied by prestaining with a mordant made of an ounce of tannic acid in a quart of water. Obviously, the vinegar concoction is rather iffy, because its strength depends on the amount of iron the liquid will absorb. Ferrous sulfate dissolved in water (about $1\frac{1}{2}$ ounces to a quart) will produce a more positive and very pleasant gray color on oak or prestained wood.

As shown in the experiment with potassium dichromate, chemicals can be used as mordants with good results, either before or after coloring the wood with plant-extract dyes (discussed below). Most plant-extract dyes are rich in various forms of tannic-acid compounds; color evolves through the reaction of such compounds to the chemical. Among the better-known chemical mordants, the top spot belongs to potassium dichromate (yellow crystals). The next most useful are copper sulfate (dark blue crystals) and ferrous sulfate (green crystals). Both of these are prepared and used like the potassium dichromate solution.

Some chemical mordants come in liquid form, such as ammonia water and hydrochloric and sulfuric acids. Use these with care and only in weak solutions—about one part chemical to a hundred parts water, though you may need to cut the solution even more. I always kept solutions of potash (potassium carbonate) and caustic soda (sodium hydroxide) handy. Again, weak solutions of these will produce interesting shades with plant-extract dyes.

Plant dyes—Until about 1870, dyes for textiles or wood were always extracted from plants, insects or animals, and rarely from minerals. For example, to obtain one pound of the dye called Tyrian purple, Mediterranean fishermen had to bring up close to four million mollusks *(Murex branderis)*, break their shells individually and carve out from their bellies the small sac that contained the coloring matter. The price of this dyestuff was so high that in ancient Rome its use was reserved by law to royalty and to the princes of the church (hence its popular name, cardinal purple). Another red dye was brewed from the female of the insect *Coccus cacti L.* Seventy thousand of these bugs had to give up their lives for each pound of dye brewed from their dried bodies. Only a hundred years ago, England imported seven million pounds of these dried insects annually.

Wood finishing as a trade was born around the turn of the century. Until then the people who worked the wood had also finished it, but the industrial revolution brought the need for specialization. To become a full-fledged cabinetmaker, a youngster had to undergo three to five years of difficult apprenticeship, often followed by a few more years of wander-learning (seeking and finding work in different towns). Business-minded bosses soon realized that women, children and second-rate workers could be trained within months to do finishing for half of the pay, and thus was born the wood-finishing trade.

We learned from our masters, the cabinetmakers, the simple dyes. I discuss several of them below. The fruit of the walnut tree, for example, is at first enveloped in a soft green cloak. As the fruit ripens, this envelope loosens and its color changes to brown; this skin becomes the source of the most popular of all dyes, the famous *brou de noix*. This is how my master's wife brewed the walnut shells: She filled a large earthenware pot with them, covered them with rainwater and added a pinch of caustic soda. Then she put on the lid. For two or three days she simmered this pot on the stove, never boiling the mixture. Finally, she strained the liquid through a linen cloth and bottled it.

A dye extracted from roasted chicory roots was not as well known as the *brou de noix* but was still quite popular. Brewing a little over a half pound of roasted chicory root in about a quart of water for a half hour yields a pleasant yellow-brown dye.

Alkanet root *(Alcanna tinctoria),* grown mainly in southern Europe, imparts a rich red color when soaked in warm mineral oil. In France, I used this dye for years and nearly always started the French polishing of mahogany by oiling up the surface of the wood with this material. Alkanet root is difficult to obtain now, but you can approximate the effect by using oil-soluble aniline dye. Dissolve the dye in lacquer thinner and then filter it through a paper towel before coloring your oil with it.

Tea, in addition to being one of the world's most popular beverages, is also an excellent dye. Use compressed tea (still available in

New York City's Chinatown) and not loose, shredded tea. A tablet of about two to three pounds of compressed tea is easily the equivalent of thirty pounds of loose leaves. By brewing this concentrated tea for several hours with a minute amount of caustic soda added to the water, I once produced a golden hue that conveyed to reproductions the warmth characteristic of fine antiques. Omit the caustic soda and the brew, properly thinned, is an excellent drink.

When combined with different chemical mordants, coloring matter extracted from various plants can provide the finisher with an infinite variety of colors. The three most important plants in my shop—available in extract form—were campeche wood (*Haematoxylon campechianum*), yellow-wood (*Cladrastis lutea*) and Brazil-wood (*Caesalpinia sappan*). Yellow-wood comes from the southern part of the United States and northern Mexico and has a definite yellow cast to it. Brazil-wood, as the name implies, comes from Brazil. In the United States I used to purchase campeche as logwood extract, or, in a more refined form, as hematine crystals or hematoxylin.

If you find some logwood, yellow-wood or Brazil-wood and want to experiment, begin by brewing 1¾ ounces to 3½ ounces of any of them in about a quart of water. Wet the wood thoroughly with the brew, and after drying apply one of the chemical mordants previously discussed to bring out the final color. Depending on the mordant, logwood produces the most beautiful blacks, grays, browns, violets and blues. Brazil-wood produces stunning reds, browns, crimsons and purples. Yellow-wood with different mordants produces bright shades of yellow, brown, olive, bronze and chestnut. Colors and shades, of course, depend not only on the colorants and mordants, but also on their concentrations. Each situation is different, and it is always best to experiment first, keeping careful records of proportions of dye and water mixed, and mordants used.

For the adventurous reader, I will list a few more color-producing plant extracts. He or she can have fun first locating the ingredients, then experimenting with the thousands of possible permutations.

The quercitron (*Quercus velutina*) is a North American tree whose bark, available in extract, will yield a yellow dye. With different mordants, it can produce yellows, olives and grays. Extract produced from the fustic tree (*Chlorophora tinctoria*) develops good yellows, browns and reds. Gall-nuts are tumors caused to grow on oak trees by small insects in many parts of the world. Try to buy the Aleppo gall, or the Smyrna gall, both of which come in fragments. These are very rich in tannin, and can produce the best black and chocolate brown. Catechu *(Acacia catechu)* is harder to find in extract, and I am not even convinced finding it would be worth the trouble. To hatch a decent color it has to be combined with logwood, yellow-wood or Brazil-wood extract. So, why bother with catechu?

Aniline dyes—Despite their romantic past, old-fashioned coloring processes have more charm than merit when compared to modern aniline dyes. In the wood-coloring trade, the future belongs to aniline dyes. They are simple, solid and dependable, easy to use and to repeat, and leave little room for error.

A little over a hundred years ago, W.H. Perkin accidentally came across the first aniline dye. Others were discovered in rapid succession, and the era of synthetic dyes began. Between the two wars, a giant color and dye manufacturing industry was born in Germany. A huge company, I.G. Farben, had almost a monopoly, and its subsidiary, Arti A.G., specialized in dyes for wood. There were no wood-coloring problems in Europe during the 1930s because Arti always had the solution. It had simple dyes that would give the selected color to nearly any wood. Other dyes involved applying a mordant followed by a dye to result in deeper penetration and more positive coloring. The most important tools in any wood-finishing shop during this period were a pharmacist's scale and a graduated glass with which to weigh and measure the proper amount of dye and water. All these dyes were properly numbered and matched to a master color chart. Arti also supplied dyes to be dissolved in alcohol or oil for special needs. Before World War II, Arti tried to gain a foothold on the American market, evidently without success, and I do not know of any manufacturer here today that markets dyes for wood with proper color samples and reliable instructions. This does not mean that American-made dyes are inferior to European ones; I simply deplore the haphazard way they are presented. The day will come, however, when American manufacturers—following Arti's example—will market good dyes backed with proper samples and concise mixing instructions. Until then we must find our way with the dyes currently available to us.

Pigments—Any solid substance that can be reduced to powder can be made into a pigment. With the proper carrier and a binder, it can become a pigmented stain. All pigmented stains have the same formula—pigment, carrier and binder. Without the binder, the pigment would precipitate out when the carrier (in which the pigment is mixed) evaporated.

Again, let me give you an example from my past. The first person who ever sought my professional help was a small-town manufacturer of a line of playpens and high chairs. The local lumber he used varied so much in color that he simply could not obtain a uniform light finish. I mixed for him equal amounts of powdered chalk and French ochre powder and stirred the mixture into a pail of lukewarm rabbit-skin glue and water. This simple stain not only solved his coloring problem, but also acted as a sealer on the wood. In this instance the chalk/ochre combination was the pigment, the water was the carrier and the glue was the binder.

The most popular and best-known pigment stains are the commercial oil colors. They contain finely ground pigments mixed into oil (the carrier) to which a drying agent is added (thus the oil becomes the binder, too). Almost always, the carrier in this mixture is extended with turpentine or other paint thinner. Although pigment stains do not actually change the color of the wood, some of the pigment remains on the wood and adds its own color to it, even after the most thorough wiping-off.

There appear to be clear-cut differences between the three ways of changing the color of the wood. The reality is far more complex. The three methods can be and very often are intermixed. My story about coloring the palazota illustrates how chemicals can be combined with synthetic dyes to create new horizons in changing the color of the wood. But that is just one story out of thousands. Chemicals can be mixed with dyes, dyes can be mixed with pigment stains and all three can be combined to improve the quality of the finished product. Nearly any stain purchased in a paint store contains pigments, dyes and some chemicals (for deeper penetration), and all do an adequate job for the amateur or even for the average professional. The old-timer sticks to chemical or natural dyes. He sometimes accepts synthetic dyes but seldom uses pigmented stains despite their great advantages and simplicity.

Application—Before using a water dye, you should first wet the wood with water to raise its grain, let it dry and sand it. However, you need a little finesse. First, you must use new, fine sandpaper that is sharp and will cut; second, your sanding strokes must not go in the direction of the grain, but on a slight bias so as not to push the fibers back into their original cradles, but to cut them off permanently. After dyeing, sand the wood with even finer paper.

A glue size is always a good thing, and color will penetrate it. You can use fairly thin hide glue, but the best is rabbit-skin glue, which is used by gilders and can be bought wherever gold leaf is sold. You must sand after every step.

Water stains, dyes and chemicals should be applied generously to the wood with a sponge. The area to be dyed should be thoroughly soaked and then the excess should be taken off with the same sponge, squeezed out, to leave the wood uniformly moist. Remember, the stronger the concentration, the more potent the stain or dye.

Some dyes, mostly the aniline dyes, can be dissolved in alcohol, oil or lacquer thinner. Therefore a liquid shellac can be further diluted and tinted with colored alcohol and the resulting colored shellac would convey a tint to the surface when applied. The same goes for lacquer—if its thinner is colored, it becomes a tinting lacquer. Wax, varnish and lacquers can be tinted with dyes dissolved in their respective thinners. They can also be "loaded," that is, some finely ground coloring matter can be mixed into them, to create a fourth way of "staining" the wood. These four ways may be compared to the four strings of a violin. The melodies one can play on these four strings are endless, but the beauty of the melody depends on the person holding the bow.

Storage—In nearly all shops I have visited, the various colored powders and materials of wood finishing are randomly stacked. Rare is the finisher who knows exactly what they are good for. The plain lampblack dry color looks exactly like the black water-soluble aniline dye, and no one can distinguish these from spirit-soluble or oil-soluble black aniline. Unless each container is clearly marked and stored with other products of the same nature, costly mistakes are bound to happen. Shelve dry colors with other dry colors, and water-soluble aniline dyes with other water-soluble aniline dyes.

In wood finishing there is no standardization of trade terms or products. French ochre dry color, for example, is nothing more than simple yellow clay, dried and finely ground. But if you buy it from three different suppliers you will receive three different shades, all called French ochre. The fourth supplier may sell it under a different label, call it "French ochre matching stain," and because of the fancy label, charge you five times the price.

The situation is far worse with dyes. The manufacturer of aniline dyes knows not about wood but about colors. He manufactures the three basic colors, red, blue and yellow, and maybe some secondary ones, and sells them to the finishing-supply houses. These dyes are clearly labeled as water, spirit or oil-soluble. Now, the finishing-supply dealer mixes the dyes to his own liking, changes the label and sells "walnut stain" (actually a walnut dye). Another manufacturer does the same thing, and the two "walnut stains" are different. Then our finishing-supply manufacturer takes matters into his own hands and mixes the spirit-soluble dye with the water-soluble one, labeling the result "walnut stain A/W" (alcohol and water soluble). Although I like my dyes to be either water, alcohol or spirit-soluble, I would not send this culprit to the guillotine—no, I would reserve this for the manufacturers who extend their dyes with sugar, starch or salt.

Until the day when pure, uniform, clearly labeled products are available, and the same name designates the same product, let us put a little organization into our own stock. Stains, dyes and pigments should be grouped together, each with its own kind. Because dry colors usually are not used frequently, your variety of these (about a pound of each) will do well on the top shelf. Right under these I keep a good assortment of a few ounces each of the aniline dyes, all alcohol-soluble only. On the same shelf, but clearly separated, I store my oil-soluble aniline dyes, again a little of each but in great variety. Underneath, on the easiest-to-reach shelves, are my aniline water dyes, one or two pounds of the frequently used colors, a few ounces of the rarely used ones. Quart cans of pigment ground in oil or in japan are on the next shelf down. On the bottom shelf I keep handy a few gallon cans of alcohol, mineral spirits and lacquer thinner, plus a batch of clean, empty containers. Also handy and not too far away is my pharmacist's scale setup. Seldom do I mix a dye without entering its number and proportions in my notebook hanging nearby.

George Frank, twenty-one years old, touches up the Lisieux branch of the Banque de France, top. Above, a group of Frank's colleagues.

Fernan Banks on Ammonia

Since no one could pronounce his name—Ferdinand Schnitzspan—his customers simply called him Fernan. We, his workers, addressed him as "Patron." He was a giant Alsatian and in the early 1920s he ran a good-sized wood-finishing shop in Paris. All his men liked him; I, then a youngster in my early twenties, loved him like a father.

This was the time when France was rebuilding after World War I, and the Banque de France was Fernan's best customer. New branch offices were being built and opened up in every important town. The furnishings of these banks were made in Paris, and Fernan had the contract to finish them. The style was always the same, the wood was invariably oak. The only allowed difference was in the finish, or more exactly, in the staining. The architect could select one of four colors, ranging from No. 1, the lightest, to No. 4, the darkest.

Early in June we shipped out all the woodwork for a bank to be installed at Lisieux, a town closer to Deauville than to Paris. This branch was supposed to open on July 16, just after the Bastille Day holiday. Around July 10 there was a big upheaval in our shop. The telephone did not stop ringing, telegrams arrived, people were coming and going like chickens without heads, and all of us sensed that something was amiss. By noon the secret was out—the Lisieux bank was stained too light. Fernan had made an error. Although his order had called for color No. 3, he made us use No. 2, a lighter one. The architect was adamant: He wanted the color he had specified and told Fernan in no uncertain terms to come and darken up the bank before the opening date.

Fernan had a car built to carry four people, but the next morning he and six of his best men somehow squeezed into it, along with all the material needed, and headed for Lisieux. We arrived around 9 A.M. and entered the bank. There was no question about the error made nor about the enormity of the task on our hands. Even if we worked twenty-four hours a day, it would still take ten to fifteen days to restain and refinish the bank. After hashing over every possibility, Fernan decided that the situation was hopeless—the job simply could not be done in the remaining few days.

There was one fellow who did not open his mouth, me, but whose mind was working furiously. Although I was the youngest and least experienced member of the group, I had more school learning than the other six combined. In evening courses I had studied wood finishing for two years. Now, as doom settled on our small company, I touched Fernan's sleeve and very timidly said, "Patron, I think I can do the job by tomorrow night."

Six pairs of eyes looked at me, not knowing whether I was joking, dreaming or trying to be funny. I explained that the job could be done by gas. If we could create a strong enough concentration of ammonia gas in the bank, there was a good chance that it would go through the thin layer of finish and react with the tannic acid in the oak to darken the wood.

Since there was no other choice, my plan was accepted. We sealed all doors, windows and openings. Then we made about thirty simple

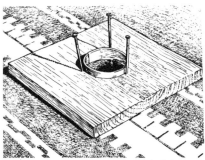

alcohol burners, consisting of a board about ten inches square, with a small bowl containing about a half pint of alcohol in the center. Three long nails held up a small pail over the bowl. With wet towels over our faces, we poured the strongest ammonia we could find into the pails, lit the alcohol and scurried out of the bank, leaving all the lights on and closing and taping up the last doors. By the time all

The type of improvised alcohol burner used to gas the Lisieux branch of the Banque de France. The three nails held up a small pail containing ammonia.

the alcohol had burned out, all the ammonia had evaporated, and there was such a concentration of gas in the room that no living thing could remain. Then we went to sleep; but no one could.

We played cards and drank an awful lot of calvados, the local apple brandy. Every hour we checked to see whether the gas was working. It was not, at least not fast enough for us to see. But the next afternoon when the architect peeked through the window, he shook his head approvingly and said, "This is it."

It was not easy to reenter the bank to get rid of the ammonia gas. We touched up the small areas unaffected by the gas, and the bank opened as scheduled.

But I was not there to see it. Fernan said to me, "You, fellow, I don't want to see for a week. Go and have a good time in Deauville." With that he stuck about a month's pay into my hand and I was on my way. On July 15 I lost my last franc at the roulette table. Luckily I had my return ticket in my pocket, and on the 16th I was back and happy at my workbench.

The Wood Finisher and the Perfect Crime

The installation of the Banque de France's branch office in St.-Nazaire, a seaport in Brittany, was a pushover. Measurements just matched; counters and dividers fit without adjustment. Despite our efforts to work at a snail's pace, progress was way ahead of schedule. We wood finishers fared even better than the cabinetmakers. Not the slightest blemish, scratch or variation in color called for our time, effort or skill.

At 3 P.M. on this particular Saturday, we crossed the street to the local bistro for our daily break. Albert Dujardin, the job foreman, announced that the bank's opening was to be postponed for a week because of problems with the complicated locking device of the huge safe door. Our holiday in St.-Nazaire would thus be extended for a full week. The good news was greeted with the enthusiastic ordering of a good bottle of wine, soon followed by another and another. It was not long before there were as many empty bottles on the table as there were men sitting at it.

Some hours later a boisterous, wobbly contingent of workers returned to the bank locker room to change into street clothes. All bade goodnight to Dujardin. As he locked up, he chuckled to himself, thinking that I, the youngest member of the crew, had certainly gotten dressed in a flash in order to get home and sleep it off. Indeed, as Dujardin had surmised, I lay in a drunken slumber, not in my bed but beneath the bank president's desk.

There I remained. It must have been 3 A.M. when the call of nature stirred me with an urgency not to be ignored. Using the night lights as a guide, I made my way across the room. "Freeze, or you die,"

From left to right, George Frank, Albert Dujardin and a Banque de France workman, photographed in the mid-1920s.

boomed a disembodied voice behind me. A steely object, a pistol, was then jammed roughly into my ribs, and I promptly collapsed, from the hangover as much as from shock.

When I opened my eyes the next morning, vague recollections of the past twenty-four hours came back to me through the symptoms of my revelry. I retraced my steps and stumbled upon three holdup men. The events of the night came back to me in a flash. Their guns were still in evidence, but no longer aimed at me. The robbers asked who I was and what I was doing in the bank. As I related the mournful tale of my misadventures, the smiles on their faces were first understanding and then patronizing. By the time I disclosed my craving for a warm bowl of milk, all four of us were laughing heartily.

Gunmen, as a rule, are not in the habit of laughing on the job, but these three were rank amateurs, professional fishermen temporarily out of work and down on their luck. One of them was the sweetheart of the waitress at the local bistro; it was from us wood finishers that she heard that an armored car, bringing the money to the new bank, would arrive Saturday night. The robbers' plan was simple: Enter the bank in the afternoon and hide, take the men with the money by surprise, lock them up, take the freshly minted money and run. It was also simple-minded. These novices did not know that the ceremony of bringing money into a new bank involved well-trained armed guards, nor that the sensitive alarm system set off a bloodcurdling warning while simultaneously alerting the police, the gendarmes and the fire department at the first indication of wrongdoing. Furthermore, not a single franc would have entered the vaults until this formidable system was working. The postponement of the opening was therefore a fortunate turn of events.

If you ever have occasion to attempt an unauthorized entry into the Banque de France, you will find that it is not an easy proposition. Gates, grills, doors and locks await you and even if you succeed at outsmarting them, the slightest false move can trigger the alarm. Our problem was no less of a feat—how to get out.

We decided to sit tight until Monday morning, when I would spirit the trio out after Dujardin opened up. This resolved, our only problem was how to kill time until our liberation. When out of my big toolbox I produced a soccer ball, the empty hall immediately resounded with the cheers of my newfound friends. We plunged ourselves into a vigorous game, which became livelier and wilder by the moment, until the inevitable occurred. The ball went careening over a cashier's cage and, landing, activated the alarm. Being the first to regain control, I took command. Retrieving the ball from behind the counter and seizing the arm of the nearest dumbstruck robber, I yelled for the others to follow. Quickly I whisked them into the employees' dressing room where, into a row of lockers, we all managed to disappear.

It was not long before we heard a flurry of activity outside the main door. Soon we heard a group of gendarmes enter the bank, ready to subdue the intruders. Finding none immediately visible, they passed the door of our dressing room to investigate further.

Needless to say, the fracas attracted Sunday churchgoers, half-dressed residents and rubberneckers. A curious crowd assembled outside, and some people entered the bank. As the scene of a crime is no place for civilians, a police chief ordered that the premises be evacuated immediately. His orders were promptly executed, and soon we four culprits found ourselves drifting anonymously into the street, right along with the crowd.

The alarm was turned off and the incident registered in the local records as the result of faulty wiring. Peace returned to St.-Nazaire. Three days later the waitress at the local bistro gave me a package and asked that I wait until I was alone to open it. It was the pistol that was to have ended my days on this planet. It could not have done so. Its hammer was missing and it wasn't loaded. I still have it as a memento of the perfect crime—the one that was never committed.

The Red Desks of the Banque de France

In Paris in 1935, the price of an office desk varied between 300 and 400 francs, and the Banque de France needed forty of them. The selection was made, the purchase order ready to be signed, when someone discovered that there were a great many desks—never used—hidden in a remote corner of the bank's huge warehouse. The bank certainly had the money for new desks, but not a single centime to spend unnecessarily. So, the order went out to bring forty desks from the warehouse to the newly remodeled section of the bank. The next day the order was carried out.

Once unpacked, the reason why the desks were never used became obvious. They had a decent shellac finish, standard at the time, but the color was ugly. The desks were made of mahogany stained red, but not a red one could live with. It was a harsh, aggressive red, a color that all the employees protested.

The purchasing agent didn't give up. He called in two wood finishers to find out if the desks could be saved at a reasonable cost. One of them was the head of a large wood-finishing outfit in Paris, and the other one had the reputation of being the best....That is how I met Agisson, my former boss, after so many years. He spoke first, telling the purchasing agent that the finish would have to be removed, the wood washed, restained and refinished. The cost would be 210 francs per desk.

Then it was my turn. I said that I might be able to change the color without removing the finish, and therefore my price would be much lower, only eighty francs per desk. I suggested that I carry out the change on one of the desks, and if it were satisfactory, I would do the same work on the remaining thirty-nine. Needless to say, Agisson was intriqued, and asked to be present when I delivered the sample desk. We all agreed. The desk was brought to my shop the same day and returned to the bank the next.

The change was obvious. All the harshness was gone, and the desk had a mellow golden-brown hue. The sample was accepted and I got the job. Agisson was puzzled. He shook my hand and with a smile said, "Of course you don't want to tell me how you did it." "Why not?" answered I. "All it took was experience and know-how."

The next day the thirty-nine desks arrived at my shop. A week later they were back at the bank and I collected my 3,200 francs—highway robbery. The job was so easy that 500 francs would have been too much. To do each desk took less than one hour, and at the time a good worker earned about seven francs per hour.

How did I do it? The secret was a type of alcohol-soluble aniline dye called auramine. A little over a quarter of an ounce dissolved in about a quart of alcohol makes a powerful golden dye that can be applied on top of most finishes with remarkable effects. Alcohol, however, applied on top of a shellac finish will burn or etch it. In fact, since alcohol is shellac's solvent, if carelessly handled the dye can simply wash off the finish instead of tinting it. If it is applied too wet, or if you happen to hit the same area two or three times, the dye will do more harm than good. So, the trick is to add ten to fifteen percent of water to the alcohol after the auramine is dissolved. The water will take out the biting teeth of the alcohol and give you far more leeway. If your strokes overlap, there is no great harm done.

On the red desks, then, I applied this dye with a handful of cotton waste, using smooth strokes. The change in color was instantaneous: The red disappeared, and the mahogany became a friendly golden-brown, easy to live with. All I had to do after applying the dye was wipe the desks clean. We did do a little extra work on the tops, applying a new coat of French polish, to be sure the auramine would be well sealed.

After forty-five years I am thinking of sending back 2,000 francs to the Banque de France as overpayment. Should I?

Questions about coloring the wood

I am making a small round extension table for a dinette, using Brazilian cherry, a fragrant wood with grain and color similar to mahogany. I would like its final color to be beige rather than ruddy brown, and it would be nice to retain the fragrance if possible.

To make a red wood blond, you have to get rid of the red. You may be able to camouflage the red and come up with a beige-brown finish by putting hints of green into the stain (if you use any), into the filler and into the finish. Or you may have to bleach the wood by washing it two or three times with the strongest chlorine bleach you can find (see also page 40). Let the wood dry between washings, sandpaper when dry and wash off with white vinegar to neutralize the bleach. If the red is gone, you are ready for staining and finishing. Peroxide bleach would surely remove the red, but would also eliminate all the beauty of your wood. Your problem is far more difficult than you realize. You must experiment on samples, don't hope for an easy solution, and be sure to treat both sides of the boards the same way. It is unlikely that you'll be able to retain the fragrance. It will not resist repeated washing, nor will it come through the finish.

My son's family is using a black-walnut trestle table that is now in its fifth gener-ation in the family. The joints are reasonably tight and the wood is sound. A com-plete restoration job is possible, but from our standpoint might detract as much as it would add. Brightening up the wood itself will be enough for us. After many years of farm use and being scoured with lye soap, and more years overhead in the attic gathering dust, it is smooth and clean but faded. I'm thinking of an oil treatment, possibly with added stain, or maybe just a good furniture polish will do the trick. But in a case like this might the resins set up and preclude further recovery of the natural color?

Your table brings a story to memory: I had an old aunt who, although she was close to ninety, was bright and alert. Her hair was white, her wrinkled face clean of cosmetics, and her whole person radiated goodness. When she died, I went to the funeral parlor for a last farewell and had a shock. Was this my aunt in the casket? The woman there had bright red cheeks, rouge on her lips, penciled eyebrows—the works. She looked like the bad woman in a Hollywood film, not like the aunt I loved.

Now back to your table. Please don't use any makeup on it. Wash it down once more with lye soap, scrub it hard and scrub it clean. Rinse it clean with water and leave it alone. If you really feel it needs protection, get some beeswax, cut shavings off it with a hand plane, fill a jar with the shavings, barely cover them with high-octane gasoline and let soak a couple of days, shaking the jar from time to time. The wax will become semi-liquid. With this wax you can coat your table, but be sure to take off all excess before it dries. When dry, bring up the shine with a wool rag and a scrubbing brush. Don't use any coloring. The beauty of your table is in the fact that it is old, worn and faded—keep it that way.

I am interested in refinishing a number of antique Chinese bamboo bird cages. All have been finished with clear varnish to show off the grain of the bamboo, which in itself is not terribly appealing to my Western eye. Can you suggest a source of infor-mation on bamboo finishing?

About fifteen years ago a large plywood company imported a few hundred sheets of bamboo plywood from Japan. They were slow sellers, and when the company decided to discontinue the line, I bought the remaining eighty panels at a discount price. I couldn't sell them either, so I used them to line a game room in my house. Feeling that clear finish would be undistinguished on bamboo, I tried to dye it, but no dye would penetrate it. Since the customer (my wife) was not insisting on the color change, I put a couple of coats of clear lacquer on, and today I am glad I did nothing more. I have learned since then that there are dyes for bamboo, but I have no personal experience with them. I am therefore giving you a hearsay tip, for whatever it's worth: Use any aniline dye that can be dissolved in acetone, and let me know how you succeed.

How do you achieve a vermilion color on wood?

Use a wood that is red (perhaps padauk) and dye it with the reddest aniline dye you can lay your hands on. After light sanding, stain it with an oil stain using vermilion mixing color diluted in mineral spirits. Seal this with shellac that has been cut and tinted somewhat with vermilion alcohol-soluble aniline dye. With the right ingredients you will obtain a vermilion color that will not change in your lifetime.

How come George Frank uses such dangerous chemicals? Why can't he do his fancy coloring with clean rainwater?

I often mention chemicals deemed dangerous. They *are* dangerous, or rather, are dangerous if misused. Gasoline is an excellent cleaning agent, but if you are lighting a cigarette while using it, your whole house may go up in smoke. Shall we stop using gasoline for cleaning? The answer is no. Use it. But be careful.

Lye and caustic soda are the two best friends of anyone copying antiques. Both of them can severely burn the skin. I've used them for five decades without trouble, wearing gloves. Many unhappy maidens wishing to die drank these and were successful. Simply don't drink them.

Gas, electricity, kitchen knives and automobiles can all become dangerous tools and may cause death if misused, yet all of us use them in our daily lives. I have used all the products I am talking about without harm simply because I use them with proper care and good ventilation. Please do likewise.

Making the Wood Colorless

Chapter Three

The Dining Room that Shed Tears

In 1930 the Baron Rotschild bought a country estate near Chantilly, a small town almost twenty miles north of Paris. He selected Maurice Lafaille, a young, poor, handsome and talented interior decorator to refurbish the chalet. Lafaille and I were pals and helped each other when the going got rough. Knowing him well, I knew that when he invited me to lunch he wanted something. When he took me to one of the best restaurants in Paris, I knew that he wanted something big.

By the time we had begun the main course, Lafaille produced a small package. When I unwrapped it I found a ball of twine about the size of a baseball. "What is it?" I asked. "Hemp, virgin hemp," replied Lafaille. "I want you to reproduce the color of this hemp on the dining-room set I just designed for the Baron Rotschild."

I learned in school and in life how to produce on wood any color of the rainbow. But because virgin hemp has no color, Lafaille stuck me with the problem of producing wood that is colorless. This I did not learn in school.

The problem was challenging, and as soon as I was back in my shop I began to experiment. First I realized that if men did not produce the color Lafaille wanted, nature did. Wood, exposed to weather, rain, snow, sun and moonlight frequently acquires a silvery whiteness, a faded, colorless quality. This is what I tried to reproduce.

The dining-room set was veneered of sawn oak, $\frac{1}{16}$ inch thick, glued with hot hide glue. First, I washed the wood clean. I mixed a fairly strong solution of caustic soda (about $1\frac{3}{4}$ ounces in a quart of water), and I soaked the wood thoroughly. Then I washed the wood with water, sponged off the excess water and waited a day or two for the wood to dry. I repeated the operation, using scrubbing brushes to get into the pores. I was not satisfied until the rinse water ran clean. Then I dried the wood. One who has never tried this method would expect the veneer to soak loose (it does not) and the wood to be rough and its pores enlarged (again this is not the case). After drying, the wood was a giant step closer to the colorlessness I was aiming for. My next step was bleaching. Had I spent as much time studying chemistry as I have spent experimenting with bleaches, I would now be an accomplished chemist. Stubbornly, I tried and tried again, hoping for the miracle that did not come.

In 1930 there were only three ways of lightening the wood. The least effective was the system combining potassium permanganate and sodium thiosulfate—it simply did not penetrate the fibers of the wood. The great champion of the bleaches was supposedly oxalic acid, but working with it for nearly five decades I have yet to bleach a surface evenly or thoroughly while using it. One of the problems is taking off the excess, the fine crystals that somehow emerge on the freshly bleached surface. If you try to wash them off, you may wind up with unevenly bleached wood. If you try to sandpaper them off, wear a gas mask and don't be surprised if the fine dust still gets through and causes you to choke. (Oxalic acid, however, is useful for antique reproductions, where the evenness of the bleaching is not so important.) The third substance for lightening the wood was chlorine bleach, better known as Clorox. Of the three, this was the most reliable, and, I would dare to say, the best.

This is what I used on the Baron's dining-room set. On the washed, dried and lightly sanded wood I applied Clorox (*Eau de Javel* in France) with a sponge, then sponged off the excess and waited. It was a sunny summer day and when the wood dried, I noticed that I was one step closer to my goal. But the bleaching process was too slow, and I wondered how I could build up the strength of the bleach. I soon learned that in France, *Eau de Javel* was available in a far more concentrated form from dealers of special chemicals. The next day I triumphantly entered my shop, carrying a large bottle of the most concentrated *Eau de Javel*. With this I breezed through the job, since two applications left the wood approximating the color of Lafaille's virgin hemp.

After the coloring came the problem of the right finish. All the horizontal surfaces of the dining set were made of one-inch thick glass, and therefore I did not have to worry about protection. I decided on an open-pore French-polish finish, made up of infinitely thin layers of white shellac. The job done, Lafaille and I delivered the set, installed it in the chalet and accepted with due modesty the Baron's compliments and a case of fine champagne. This was in midsummer of 1930, and it was much like a midsummer night's dream. It did not last long. About six weeks later, Lafaille entered the shop visibly upset, shouting, "George, the dining room is crying!" Further discussion disclosed that Lafaille had received a telephone call from the Baron, who told him that the dining-room set was shedding tears—drops of water were running down everywhere, without visible cause. An hour later we arrived in Chantilly to find that every word was true. Water was coming from the wood. But how? Why?

Debating all possibilities, the Baron, Lafaille and I reached a verdict. The bleach cried. The concentrated *Eau de Javel* saturated the wood with chlorine and when the water evaporated, the solids stayed in the wood. Chlorine has a great affinity for water and will absorb a great deal of moisture from the air when the air is moist. The wood did not cry during the dry days of summer, but only with the humid, rainy days of early fall. Somehow I had to neutralize the chlorine on the wood. First I washed the wood down with a solution of acetic acid, but there was a film of shellac on the wood and the acetic acid could not penetrate it. Then I tried oxalic acid.

People who claim to know recommend dissolving the acid in warm water in a nonmetallic container and applying it either with a sponge or a brush without metal. I dissolved the acid in alcohol and applied it with a wad of cotton, with no significant change in effect. I filled a jar halfway with acid and then poured alcohol in until the jar was almost full. (The alcohol absorbs as much acid as it can, thus becoming a saturated solution. The acid the alcohol can't hold remains in crystals at the bottom of the jar.)

I applied the acid carefully, wiping off the excess with soft cloths, to neutralize the chlorine through the shellac. This process produced unpleasant gases and I had to proceed with great caution and much ventilation. Care, patience and perseverance helped me to correct the problem of the crying dining-room set, and in about a week's time I restored it to its original beauty, eliminating the cause of its tears.

On Peroxide Bleach

There is no doubt in my mind that the leaders in wood finishing in the 1930s were the Germans, so when a manufacturer from a small town in Germany agreed to pay my fare and my fee for solving a finishing problem, I went without hesitation. The problem turned out to be so childishly simple that I was ashamed to keep the fee and donated most of it to a worthy charity. The balance I spent to visit the famous Leipzig Fair. One of the major exhibitors there was Arti A.G., the company that supplied Europe with all the dyestuff the woodworking industry could possibly need.

Arti A.G. treated their foreign customers with warm hospitality. Because I was one of their better foreign customers, I was invited into the workroom attached to their exhibition booth, to munch on snacks and drink some excellent beer. While I was there, my host upset a container of walnut stain, along with a primitive sand-timer made of unfinished white wood. This quickly soaked up the dark stain. After cleaning up the mess, my host picked up the sand-timer and raised his finger, signaling me to watch. From a shelf he took down a bottle and poured a bit of its contents into a beaker. From another bottle he added a few drops to the beaker, and then he dipped in the stained sand-timer. To my amazement, the stain disappeared and the wood became as white as it had been before. This was the first time I realized the potential of hydrogen peroxide as a bleach.

When I returned to Paris, I went to Rhone-Poulenc, the leading dealer in chemicals, where I learned that hydrogen peroxide is measured by volume. The kind we purchase to disinfect wounds is one of the ten to twelve-volume variety. The kind used to clean the sand-timer was of either the 100 or 130-volume kind. The drops added from the second bottle were plain ammonia. I also learned that the highly concentrated hydrogen peroxide was unstable, and contact with any other chemical or even dirt provoked its decomposition. The volatility of concentrated hydrogen peroxide could be moderated, however, with a white powder known as acetanilide. About half an ounce of this per quart of hydrogen peroxide calmed down the excitable bleach. From then on, I had a sort of peroxide pipeline to the warehouse of Rhone-Poulenc. I bleached as no wood finisher ever did before. I did not invent this manner of bleaching, but I used as much peroxide as all the other wood finishers in Paris combined.

Variations of this bleach, called albino bleach and one-two bleach in the trade, are standard in industry today. Thousands of gallons are used daily. Scientific books praise its value, yet none mention its fatal shortcomings. Yes, it bleaches the wood; yes, it obliterates color; yes, it makes the wood white like paper, white like the color of a dead person's cheeks; but it completely kills all markings of the wood. I don't use peroxide bleach any longer, and I am sorry I ever did.

My wife and I once visited a prefinished-panel factory near Philadelphia. Oceangoing ships were docked fifty feet from the machinery that did the finishing. Huge cranes lifted bundles of unsanded $\frac{1}{8}$-inch thick panels from the bowels of the ships and landed them gently near a conveyor belt. The straps were cut and machinery took over. Air suction lifted up the first panel, and it was on its way to becoming whatever the customer wanted.

Sanding was the first operation, done in tunnels from which the panels emerged smooth and dust-free. This was followed by filling and undercoating, again done in tunnels. The panels emerged at that point looking like light-brown paper, and not the slightest markings of the original wood were visible. That is when the finishing began. Huge rollers produced artificial pores, knots or other markings. The panels were scored. Then another series of rollers painted on the desired colors. Drying tunnels made them ready for the next operation. The panels were lacquered, rubbed, waxed, counted, strapped and loaded onto trucks. The machinery and equipment took up roughly the area of two football fields and produced a completely finished panel every five seconds.

Of this narrative the two facts to remember are: The surfaces of the panels to be finished were transformed into completely neutral, paperlike areas, and the grain and markings of the original wood had nothing to do with the final finish. Now back to the peroxide. Peroxide will bring wood to uniform paleness, and pigmented stains, tinted lacquers and fake antiquing combined will result in a pleasing, salable finish, the production of which is closer to the printing process of the panels than to real wood finishing. With very few exceptions, a fine wood finisher has no use for peroxide bleach.

Questions about bleaching and removing paint from wood

I have come across a sideboard (pecan veneer) that has had a red candle set on it and lit. The wax melted and ran down the side to the bottom, leaving a ring of wax on the lacquered surface. After trying a number of things, I came to the conclusion that the wax had penetrated the top coat. Do you have any suggestions other than stripping the entire surface?

Before stripping your sideboard, try the following remedies: Fill a small jar about halfway full of oxalic acid and cover it with water—almost to the top of the jar. Shake the jar frequently and twenty-four hours later, try to bleach the spots. It may work. Or try to bleach the spots with Clorox. Use 600-grit wet-and-dry paper, using the Clorox instead of water. A thorough soaking of the spotted areas with plain gasoline may increase the effectiveness of both these bleaching methods.

I recently inherited a solid oak roll-top desk from my grandfather and of course there is an ink stain on the writing surface. Are there any successful methods for removing or bleaching ink stains from oak?

Sorry, I don't know of any chemical that would tracelessly eliminate the ink-spots. The only way to do it would be through scraping and sandpapering.

If I did know about some magic chemical I would be loath to give it to you. To my mind a modern desk with inkspots is dirty, but an old desk without inkspots is not an old desk. You are lucky to have your grandpa's desk—leave the inkspots alone.

I have come into possession of an old dentist's tool cabinet made from oak. The original finish was stain and varnish, but it has since been given a coat of green, then white, paint. My previous attempts at stripping oak have resulted in the wood turning gray. Can you recommend a stripping material, either manufactured or homemade, that will not discolor the wood?

Generally speaking, there are two kinds of paint removers, the flammable type and the nonflammable type. I advise you to use the flammable type because nonflammable remover may contain strong chemicals such as lye or caustic soda. These will not only attack, soften and remove the finish coatings, but also may attack the wood itself and certainly the dyes or stains that were used on it. The flammable type will attack, weaken and remove only the finish. It will have no effect on the wood or the dye on the wood. Do a thorough job and, if you care to, do a final wash with lacquer thinner and/or alcohol.

Changing the Tactile
Quality of the Wood

Chapter Four

The tactile quality of wood that comes straight from the lumberyard may satisfy a rough carpenter for use in rafters or boat landings, but it certainly will not please the fine woodworker. The woodworker almost always wants the lumber as smooth as possible or, conversely, rough, rugged or coarse-looking in order to convey a desired personality.

Shortly after World War II, I traveled through Alaska. In Wrangell, I was given a guided tour of the local high school by its principal, a native Indian. I complimented him on how well the woodworking shop was equipped and on how intelligently young Eskimos and Indians were being initiated into the trade. He in turn complained that the scope of their possibilities was limited, since they had available only native Alaskan wood, excellent for construction, but rather poor for more refined projects. I asked for and was granted permission to use the shop after school. The next day I presented six or eight beautiful samples of various woods to the principal, who exclaimed: "Oh, if we had lumber like this we also could build masterpieces." All my samples, of course, were made of lumber that I had scrounged from the school shop or the local lumberyard. The difference was in the tactile quality. My samples were sandpapered to perfection, revealing all the beauty of the grain, the existence of which had been ignored by teachers and pupils alike.

To make the wood smooth, cabinetmakers use planers, planes and scrapers. Furthermore, sandpapering the wood is technically the cabinetmaker's or carpenter's job: The work should be handed to the finisher already finely sanded with a grit of 100 to 150. Except in cases where the wood is made deliberately rough, the finisher uses a complete arsenal of tools, skills and materials to make the wood even smoother, and eventually to bestow a mirrorlike appearance upon it. In this chapter I will take you step by step to the mirror finish, which I think is the best in the world.

Sanding

Sanding is the first step leading to a good finish. In the wood finisher's tool kit, the finest grades of sandpaper are most important. While the woodworker rarely needs to use sandpaper beyond 150 grit, the wood finisher seldom needs paper rougher than 120 grit.

Sandpaper, as the name implies, is nothing but abrasive glued to paper. With progress, however, all three ingredients have been improved tremendously. The paper today is highly sophisticated, and made for the purpose of sandpapering alone; the sand has been replaced by particles of garnet, aluminum oxide or silicon carbide; and these abrasive particles are fused to the paper electronically. Some sandpaper—wet-and-dry paper—is waterproof.

To determine the merits of each type of sandpaper, a testing laboratory is necessary. Until such scientific testing disproves my choices, I'll continue to rely on open-coat silicon-carbide paper, which, although more expensive than the other two types, is harder and cuts faster. The terms *open-coat* and *closed-coat* refer merely to the density of the particles deposited on the surface of the paper. Open coat has about fifty percent coverage, closed coat has a hundred percent coverage. Closed coat will cut faster, but it has a tendency to clog up, especially on soft wood.

Sandpaper must always be sharp. I pity the wood finishers who rub two sheets of 100-grit sandpaper together and expect to achieve the smoothness of a 120-grit or 150-grit paper. Instead, they get dull 100-grit paper. Throw away sandpaper when it becomes dull, but remember that clogged sandpaper and dull sandpaper are not the same thing. You can unclog sandpaper with a brush, with compressed air and also with the simple sandpaper-cleaning fluids that are often advertised in trade magazines.

Frank was called in to remedy a thorny finishing problem on this bird's-eye maple dining-room set manufactured in 1930 by Rambaudi, Dantoine & Cie, Lyons, France. The set is inlaid with ebony and an alloy of brass and zinc—sanding carried the ebony powder over the milk-white maple, maple powder over the ebony and metal powder over both. The solution was simple: Frank blew the dust out of the pores with compressed air. Then he sprayed the wood with a sealer coat of shellac. He used an air gun such as is used by graphic artists and though this technique raised quite a few eyebrows (sprayed finishes were unknown at the time), the system worked and Frank earned his fee.

The efficiency of sandpaper can be increased slightly by using the right sanding block. For instance, for the smoothest possible sanding, I use a marble block measuring 2½ inches by four inches and about one inch thick, perfectly flat on the bottom. I stretch a single sheet of fresh 400-grit wet-and-dry paper over it. I use water for this final sanding, which not only acts as a lubricant but also raises the grain. I sand not with the grain but on a slight bias, in order to cut off the raised grain instead of pushing it back.

When sanding projects such as checkerboards, dark-colored dust may get into the pores of the lighter-colored wood. There is no reason, however, why this dust must remain there unless some adhesive like improperly cleaned-off glue is involved. It can be simply blown or sucked away, or brushed off. Compressed air may be needed, but a good vacuum cleaner ought to do the job.

Filler

Sanding may eliminate most of the asperities from the surface of the wood but because the wood has pores, in many cases fairly large ones, sandpaper alone cannot make the wood absolutely smooth. Filling the pores is the next step in attaining a perfect finish.

The first requisite of a filler, in normal use, is that it be as inconspicuous as possible. Later on I will talk about filling the pores decoratively, when we want the filler to be distinct from the wood, but that process is an exception. In a well-executed French-polished finish, for example, the pores are barely discernible. (On page 60 I describe the classic method of filling the pores in French polishing, in which rubbing the wood with pumice yields microdust that conveys the perfect coloring to the pumice. The professional finisher, when French polishing dark mahogany, will replace the pumice with powdered brick, and when working with ebony, will add powdered charcoal to the pumice.)

The filler, in addition to being inconspicuous, must fill the pores well and permanently. Some fillers are based on starches, but we had better leave them to the Oriental craftsmen, who don't seem to mind that these fillers shrink. They are willing to apply ten to twenty coats of filler to achieve the desired smoothness. We Westerners are more demanding, more in a hurry, so our industry has developed fillers that, when correctly applied, will fill the pores well, shrink little and stay put. The formula is simple. Filler is a powdered mineral that is mixed (not dissolved) in a carrier liquid and a binder. The powdered mineral can be fine sand, silica, talcum powder, powdered brick or a mixture of these; the carrier can be mineral spirits, oil, alcohol or water; the binder can be glue, varnish, shellac or asphaltum. In theory, once the wood is filled, the carrier evaporates, leaving the powder in the pores. Without the binder, the powder would remain just that—powder. The binder binds the particles together and also binds them to the wood. The smaller the pores of the wood, the finer the powder in the filler must be. For small pores, the filler should also be more liquid and less pastelike.

In the olden days we wood finishers made our own filler. Today I would not. Manufacturers of commercial fillers have access to minerals so finely ground that we cannot buy the likes of them by the pound. They also have far more complicated measuring and mixing equipment. Furthermore, commercial fillers come in many colors, matching any wood that you care to use. (To select the right filler, choose the color closest to the wood to be filled and experiment with scrap; if the wood is dyed, select a filler matching the dyed wood.) For old time's sake, however, I will give you a few old-timer's fillers.

For natural oak, smash to powder in a mortar about a pound of rosin (colophony). Soak this powder overnight in about two quarts of mineral spirits. In another container, mix about four pounds of whiting powder and a pound of French ochre powder, then mix the contents of the two containers well. You have now a primitive, yet fairly efficient, filler. The colored whiting is the mineral, the rosin is the binder and the mineral spirits is the carrier.

For a filler for dark oak, thin down asphaltum paint (which is the consistency of heavy molasses) with mineral spirits until it is free-flowing, and mix in whiting just until the filler becomes the consistency of heavy cream. This also can be used on walnut or, with the addition of a proper dry color, on rosewood. Here the asphaltum is the binder and mineral spirits is the carrier.

Lazy French-polishers (or those looking for shortcuts) mix talcum powder with dry colors (to match the color of the wood to be finished), thin this down with alcohol (carrier) and add some liquid shellac (binder). The more shellac, the harder it is to take the excess off, but the better it sticks to the wood and fills the pores. This is quite a tricky filler, definitely not for amateurs.

To fill wood having small pores, the finisher in the old days painted on a concoction of glue-water (carrier and binder) mixed with some fine powder such as chalk or talcum colored to suit. When the water evaporated, the powder and glue kept the wood well sealed. Fine sanding left the wood ready for finishing.

Some woods (such as birch, beech, maple and sycamore) have pores so insignificantly small that there is no reason to use filler on them. It would be extra work, with no worthy improvement of the smoothness of the wood. These seemingly poreless woods, however, frequently do have microscopic hairlike fibers that rise up when in contact with water, affecting the surface smoothness of the wood. Therefore, on small-pored woods, I would use a sealer rather than a filler. A sealer will either hold the hairlike fibers down or hold them up for whisking away with fine sandpaper.

My favorite sealer is made from rabbit-skin glue. This glue, sold mainly for use by gilders, comes in thin sheets measuring about six inches square. It must be soaked first in water for a day or two before being cooked in fresh water. Let the warm glue soak into the wood, wipe or sponge off the excess and allow to dry. Then sandpaper with 150 or 200-grit paper and start on the finish.

If rabbit-skin glue is not available, regular hide glue will do. You could also use thinned-down shellac or varnish (about a third to two-thirds thinner) or plain lacquer sealer. Don't forget to sand following application. The glue sealer does not have to be repeated, but all the others should be. Remember that if you intend to dye the wood, this must be done before sealing.

Remember also to dye the wood before filling. Providing the dye and the filler have different solvents, you will have no problem with the filler restaining the wood. The best dyes are water-based and ninety-five percent of all fillers are oil-based. However, if you choose to use an oil-based or alcohol-based dye, you will have to seal the dyed wood before applying the filler. The best sealer is a wash coat of shellac, but a thin coat of lacquer or lacquer sanding sealer will do the job, too. Sandpaper, of course, should be ever present and always used. To thin and apply the filler, follow the instructions on the can to the letter.

Remember that filler belongs only in the pores of the wood. You must take great care to clean the filler from the surface of the wood or else it will do the exact opposite of what it was intended to do and make the wood less smooth. There is another good reason to clean off the filler. It has an abrasive action, and while we are rubbing this abrasive into the pores and rubbing the excess off, we are simultaneously improving the tactile quality of the wood. Hard rubbing with rags and 3/0 or 4/0 steel wool should take all the excess from where it does not belong.

On projects involving several different woods (such as backgammon boards) where you cannot use paste filler, sanding sealer and lacquer make a good substitute filler. There is a tricky way to do this. First, spray a fairly heavy coat of sanding sealer on the wood, let dry and sandpaper smooth. Next, spray a thin coat of clear lacquer on the wood, let dry and repeat with alternating coats of sealer and lacquer until the pores are filled. From then on, build up the finish with layers of clear lacquer.

To make a putty for filling imperfections in the wood, mix the fine sawdust from the wood you are using with hide glue or with white glue, or mix it with shellac or clear lacquer. (The combination of sawdust and lacquer is well known under the trade name Plastic Wood.) To fill small holes in the wood, such as those made for countersunk nails, after finishing is complete melt equal quantities of beeswax and paraffin wax in a double boiler. Add dry powdered colors. Then, for every ounce of wax, add a drop of linseed oil. You can make small paper tubes with one end closed and pour the well-stirred liquid into them. The oil will keep the wax malleable.

Finishing Materials

After filling, the next step, though not the last, is coating the wood with finishing products. Although we seem to have a great variety of these, in the final analysis we do not. I will give a brief description of each of the readily available finishes.

Wax—The earliest finishes were the waxes and the oils. Wax, in its most popular form, is produced by bees. It does not need much refining. Heat will melt it; mineral spirits, gasoline and turpentine will dissolve it; and it's ready to be used.

In the olden days we purchased beeswax in the shape of small bricks. We made shavings of it with a roughing plane, filling an earthen jar with them. Then we covered the shavings with turpentine and left them to melt, stirring the mixture frequently with a wooden stick. When melted, the wax was like heavy cream—neither liquid nor paste. In time the turpentine was replaced by faster-drying solvents, byproducts of petroleum refining. The most frequently used solvent today is mineral spirits to which a bit of industrial perfume (such as pine oil or citronella) has been added to mask the smell.

Questions about wax

What finishing techniques are recommended for solid wood kitchen countertops? My objectives are durability and avoiding food poisoning and staining.

Would you apply today's technology—as ninety-five percent of kitchen designers do—you would cover most of your countertop with plastic laminate. This will ensure prevention against food stains and food poisoning as well as provide an extremely resistant surface. You could then reserve an area about twenty-four inches square in your countertop (or anywhere else in your kitchen for that matter) for a butcher block. This could be either the commercial variety from the lumberyard or the professional type, which uses end-grain maple as the working surface. For finishing, buy some paraffin wax (the kind mother used to seal her fruit preserves) and melt it. Coat your block with this melted wax. It will gel quite quickly. Then, with a dull scraper, scrape off as much of the wax as you can. The remaining thin coat will offer a safe, protective coating to your butcher block. Repeat the process as the need arises.

I finished my butcher block with polyurethane varnish. For the first coat, I used three parts thinner to one of varnish. I applied this mixture generously to all sides of the block, let sit for about ten minutes, then rubbed vigorously

Wax can be used all by itself to finish wood, or it can add its satiny shine to other finishes. The old-timer frequently applied a few coats of fairly thin shellac to the wood (sanding between coats), then applied the wax on top of these coatings. Wax, like all finishing materials, gains if applied in thin coats rather than in heavy ones. Three thin coats of wax will give a better finish than one heavy coat. After applying each coat, rub off the excess enthusiastically with burlap before it dries. The solvent evaporates fairly fast, and the film of wax remaining on the wood can be rubbed or brushed with a wool rag or a soft brush to a satiny shine. By repeating the waxing, you will build up a layer of wax on the wood that is almost impermeable.

Beeswax is soft, however, and because it never really hardens through, it doesn't resist abrasion very well. But don't sell wax short. Beeswax, in both natural and bleached forms, can be supplemented with other, harder waxes. Mineral waxes, such as paraffin or

---

with a rough cloth. I let the butcher block dry overnight, then brushed on two coats of dilute varnish (about two parts varnish to one part thinner). I didn't rub them off. This produced a thin but solid coating.

We have a rosewood-veneered tabletop that was waxed but developed a black ring four inches in diameter when water leaked onto it around a silver vase. Having used salad oil to remove white water marks, I tried this, but to no avail. Since the blemish apparently contains silver oxide, I also tried silver polish, which did nothing. Perhaps I'm not penetrating the waxed surface. Because the stain is dead center, I hesitate to use bleach, and because it's on a veneered surface, I suspect it's too deep to rub out. Any ideas?

The first thing to do is to clean the tabletop of all finish. Wax is hard to eliminate, and you'll have to do this in several steps. Soak the tabletop with gasoline, then wipe the melted finish off with rags. Repeat this several times, until you think the tabletop is clean. Then wash it two or three times more, only this time use lacquer thinner instead of gasoline. Be careful to ventilate your work area well.

Next, scrub your table with warm water and laundry detergent until it is free of wax, wiping the excess water off constantly. The spot should be gone. If it still persists, however, use a wire brush measuring two inches by seven inches that has 1¾-inch long wires. Wet the wood and wipe up the excess

ozocerite (also called ceresine) and vegetable waxes, such as carnauba or candelilla, are combined in modern paste waxes. Again, with rare exceptions, commercial waxes are so good that they give you no reason to try to blend your own. Moreover, it is quite dangerous to do so. In Paris, my foreman's wife lost her life trying to make wax.

Nevertheless, for the adventure-bent finisher, here is a formula for an excellent wax. Melt with the proper care in a double boiler (never directly over the source of heat) equal quantities of beeswax, ozocerite and carnauba waxes. You can add to this combination one part paraffin wax or, if you can find any, montan wax (a hard mineral wax). When the wax is melted, far away from any source of flame or spark, add to it mineral spirits scented with about two percent pine oil. The quantity of the mineral spirits should be approximately four to five times that of the molten wax. Emulsified wax, which is described on page 115, is another excellent wax finish.

Wire brushes should be rotated in a tumbling motion, like that of a turning wheel.

moisture. Then brush the damp wood in the manner shown in the drawing above, sweeping with the grain of the surface. Some of the wires will reach into the bottom of the pores, and if you get the knack, will kick out all unwanted material.

Now, if the spot is still there, start with chemicals—first, simple Clorox. If this doesn't work, dissolve oxalic acid in alcohol and, using rubber gloves, wipe the spot off. If either the Clorox or oxalic acid eliminates the spot, neutralize the wood with a vinegar wash. Under no circumstances use peroxide bleach. If neither the Clorox nor the acid works, I would dig into my vocabulary of Hungarian swear words and reveneer the tabletop.

Oil—The seed of the flax plant gives us linseed oil. Raw linseed oil contains portions of oil that will never dry, but when the oil is refined through steam-heating and metallic drier compounds are added, the boiled linseed oil so produced is an excellent and easy-to-use finish. All we need do is spread the oil generously over the surface to be finished, let it soak in for fifteen to thirty minutes, and wipe off the excess energetically, preferably with burlap. An extremely thin coat of oil will remain behind to undergo a chemical change—it will harden, or cure. The longer the curing time, the harder the oil becomes. Two weeks to a month is the usual drying time a craftsman should allow before recoating. Each additional coat adds an extra film, and rub-

Questions about oil

We have a fine old grand piano with a crazed varnish finish. An old piano tuner told me to feed the old finish with boiled linseed oil thinned with paint thinner. This went well for the first two applications. After the third, it would not dry to the feel of a finish that could be sanded. It's been four months and it is soft but not tacky. Where do I go from here?

There are only three ways to cope with an old finish: Remove it completely and refinish; clean it and apply a sealer so the new finish is never actually in contact with the old; and the way you chose, the riskiest of all, to add a finish that would melt into the old one. This can only be done if you know what the old finish was, and even then it is hazardous because you don't know what it has been cleaned with or what traces remain on the wood.

At this point I would try some experiments. First, wash the finish with gasoline. Be careful, make sure to ventilate well and allow no chance of fire. Soak an area well, wipe it dry a few minutes later, and by next morning the softness may be gone. Second, with a wet Brillo pad, wash and rub an area and wait overnight. If neither trick works, you'll have to strip the finish off and start over.

I'd like your opinion on using mineral oil instead of linseed oil to treat and protect wood. I don't know anything about mineral oil except that it is highly refined (edible) petroleum, it doesn't stink and it's available in three weights. Thus mineral oil could be a terrific treatment for salad bowls and tabletops. On the other hand, if

bing with burlap (which acts as an abrasive) makes the surface smoother and smoother. Oiling can be repeated ad infinitum, and a very pleasant finish will build up in time. But linseed oil never hardens through completely, and therefore offers rather limited protection. To overcome this, I add up to twenty-five percent each good-quality varnish and turpentine to the oil. This makes the curing time shorter and the film tougher.

Throughout the years I have heard of various "heirloom" finishes consisting of combinations of oils and other finishing materials, most of them handed down from grandparent to grandchild. One such finish calls for mixing one part boiled linseed oil, one part turpentine

---

it's so terrific, how come no one uses it? When my furniture gets its seasonal linseed oiling, the house plain stinks.

Boiled linseed oil to which you add about five percent japan drier will offer far greater protection to wood than mineral oil. The correct method to use linseed oil has much to do with the final result. The oil-drier mixture should be applied generously and left fifteen to thirty minutes on the wood so it can penetrate well. Then, as much oil as possible should be taken off by rubbing the wood with rags, hard. The oiled surface should be given ample time (a week at least) to dry. You repeat this five or six times and you build up a fine protective shield on your wood, which, because of the repeated rubbing, also becomes pleasantly smooth. True, linseed oil does not compete with Chanel No. 5 for pleasant smell, but the smell goes away with proper drying and hardening. Mineral, or paraffin, oil will not harden and I would never use it as a protective coating.

I have been making a few small projects using cherry wood and finishing them with oil. My problem is the end grain. I get it very smooth, yet the oil seems to creep out after I have rubbed it with a cloth, leaving small shiny specks.

Since your problem is the fact that the end grain absorbs more finishing oil than the flat surface does, the remedy is to seal the end grain before applying the oil. For sealer I would use fairly thin glue-water. Rabbit-skin or plain hide glue could be used, although if these are not readily available you can buy at the drugstore some gum arabic, or some gum tragacanth, and brew it in

---

and one part melted beeswax. Another calls for mixing boiled linseed and white shellac. To these I say: *Ne sois pas plus royalist que le roi* (don't be more royalist than the king himself). Wax, shellac and linseed oil are all old proven finishes. Mix them and you are looking for trouble.

More and more woodworkers feel that the days of finishing with boiled linseed oil are numbered. They feel that the oil extracted from the fruit of the tung tree (*Aleurites cordata*) is far superior in both moisture resistance and film hardness. This tree grows mainly in Japan and in Formosa. The Chinese variety (*Aleurites fordii*) grows on the mainland of China, though it is also cultivated in the southern part of the United States, Brazil and Argentina.

The protective qualities of tung oil have long been appreciated: In

warm water. My guess is that one ounce in a quart of water will give you the right proportion, but try it out first on scrap. Use the sealer lukewarm, seal the end grain with it, let it dry, sandpaper it fine and apply the oil. Be careful, don't leave any sealer on the flat part.

I have constructed a dining-room table of walnut and walnut veneer over Novaply. It is good looking but won't stay that way if we keep using it. The linseed-oil finish can't take hot and cold or moisture. Is there a finish I can apply over the oil that will take everyday use? Or could I strip the oil and apply epoxy resin?

Before refinishing with a modern polyurethane varnish, first remove the linseed. Here is how: Soak the wood with lacquer thinner and wipe off with a clean rag. Repeat several times, until the thinner has nothing more to dissolve, using a small, stiff brush to reach into corners. The success of your refinishing depends on how clean the wood is. Scrub it down thoroughly with water and brown soap or laundry detergent. This may leave the grain slightly raised, so use 150 or 200-grit sandpaper to make it smooth again, and brush off the dust. The pores of the wood will still be sheltering minute particles of the old finish. I wouldn't attempt any further cleaning; I would rather seal them in there. For sealer, use a well-diluted solution of your new finish or use commercial shellac, orange for dark wood and white for light, diluted one part to four of alcohol. Let dry twenty-four hours or more, sand and you are ready to apply new stain and finish—the wash coat of shellac won't interfere with either.

fact, some historians attribute the preservation of the Great Wall of China to a tung coating. For centuries, varnishes have had tung oil as one of their main ingredients, and its use is steadily expanding. Nowadays tung oil is also found in printing inks, oilcloth, linoleum and wire insulation, and as a waterproofing agent for paper and textiles. About ten or fifteen years ago, tung was introduced to the wood-finishing trade and its acceptance was unanimously enthusiastic.

The use of tung is simplicity itself. Spread a coat on the surface to be finished, wait about fifteen minutes and clean off all excess. What remains will dry into a remarkably pleasing and protective film. The process can be repeated, but, as with all film-producing finishes, sanding between coats is essential.

Also on the market today and in wide use are a number of penetrating oils under various trade names. These are mixtures of oils, varnishes and driers in proprietary proportions, and only laboratory testing can determine the relative merits of each.

Shellac—While waxes and oils, rubbed finishes, yield good results, many wood finishers prefer built-up finishes, such as are possible with lacquer and varnish. Some finishers also use shellac, applying it with a brush, to produce a built-up finish. For centuries shellac was the king of all finishes, durable and beautiful. Were finishes rated for their protective qualities, shellac would rate far better than the average. However, because shellac's solvent is alcohol, it follows that shellac is vulnerable to alcohol, and many a fine shellac finish has been ruined by careless drinkers. The advantage of such a finish is its comparatively fast drying time, which allows quick recoating. Shellac, however, has a short shelf life once dissolved, and metal containers further shorten its useful life span. Aged, metal-contained shellac frequently will not dry properly and can cause grave problems.

You can generally avoid these problems if you make your own liquid shellac, which is easy to do in the shop. Shellac for wood finishing comes in four types: flakes ("superfine" is best), buttons, bleached and granulated. I assume only good-quality shellac is bleached, but it will never dry as hard as unbleached will. The shellac that gave me the best results was the button kind, about three inches in diameter and about $\frac{1}{8}$ inch thick. I always used plain, denatured alcohol as a solvent. Three or four pounds of shellac per gallon of alcohol is generally about right.

I have heard of wood finishers having problems dissolving a new type of shellac—refined, dewaxed, powdered shellac—in alcohol. I see no reason for using this type of shellac, as the old-fashioned types work dependably and well. In Paris we did our own dewaxing, in a loose sense of the word. We strained the concentrated liquid shellac through filter paper, which arrested the waxy substance but let through the clear liquid. We used this exclusively on moldings and carvings where French polishing was difficult.

The beauty of the finish shellac produces in French polishing, though hard to achieve, is unparalleled. For this reason, French polishing is usually confined to fine, luxury items or high-quality reproductions. Although I am a good French-polisher and remember fondly the beautiful finishes I achieved with shellac, I am convinced that with the advent of modern lacquers and varnishes, the heyday of shellac is over. Nevertheless, should you wish to try your hand at French polishing, here is some information.

In the first place, no filler is used in the traditional way of French polishing. A large part of French polishing is working pumice stone into the surface of the wood, using a special pad that English crafts-

Questions about shellac

As a first venture into cabinetmaking, I constructed several pieces of bedroom furniture from pine. These pieces were treated first with a petroleum-base stain (Fletco Varathane Danish Walnut), and then given eight coats of white shellac. The pieces were then paste-waxed. The problem is that cloudy marks have formed on several of the pieces. Can you tell me what caused this? Also, is there some way to remove these cloudy marks without having to sand off the original finish and start again?

Your stain was probably not properly dry when you started to apply the finish. The cloudiness may also come from the shellac, which often does not keep well when dissolved. Ready-made shellac—even if it comes from a good manufacturer—may take too long to dry or may not harden completely, and coats applied without proper drying periods in between may become muddy or cloudy.

Try this for a remedy. Mix half a gallon of gasoline and a pint of mineral oil. Take some wet-and-dry 220-grit paper and sand the whole job thoroughly, using the gasoline mixture generously as a lubricant, in a well-men call a rubber and French craftsmen call a tampon. The heart of this tampon is made of wool from old socks or sweaters. The role of the wool is to hold and to release slowly the alcohol (mixed with a trace of shellac), and later shellac only. The wool is wrapped in a porous fabric—linen is best if you can find any—which covers it snugly and smoothly. The tampon, about the size and shape of an egg, should fit the inside of your palm, where you will hold it quite firmly. The bottom side of the tampon becomes quite flat, as it slides and slides on the surface of the wood.

As you French polish, you feed the wool with a few drops of alcohol at a time, and you sprinkle some finely ground pumice on the surface to be polished. In the olden days, we used to put pumice powder in cloth bags that were each about the size of a golf ball. The cloth acted as a strainer, letting through only the desired grade of pumice. At successive stages, the wood finisher would use cloths with smaller and smaller openings.

Then, with broad circling motions, you begin to force the pumice into the pores. The pumice will fill up the small spaces of the linen and since it is an abrasive substance, will cut off invisibly small par-

---

ventilated area. Concentrate on the cloudy areas. Wipe dry. Wash the job down a second time with clean gasoline. Wipe and dry again. Now apply one or two thin coats of fresh shellac (one pound per gallon). Let it dry. Steelwool and wax, and hope for the best.

I would like to finish birds carved in vermilion wood without darkening the bright color. Is shellac a good choice of finish?

The answer lies not with the finish material, but with the tricky way of applying it. My choice would be fresh white shellac, but you can use picture varnish or water-white lacquer. The trick is to get the finishing material to contact the wood and dry at the same time, so the carrying agent (alcohol, thinner or turpentine) has no time to enter the pores of the wood and darken it. I would use an air brush of the type commercial artists use or a mouth sprayer, which you can buy for a couple of dollars at an art-supply store. Regulate it to spray as much air and as little finish as possible, and hold it far from the work. The first coat must be light and thin. Successive

ticles of the wood. Together these will slowly fill up the pores under the rubbing of your fists. Because the pumice carries with itself the finest possible wood dust, it takes on the color of the wood. It thus becomes invisible, practically part of the wood itself. This is the finest method of filling wood. Not all French polishers, however, go through this slow and tiring process. They use various kinds of fillers, as discussed on page 49.

When all the pores of the wood are filled, by whatever method, increase the amount of shellac in the tampon, and slowly begin to build up a film of shellac on the wood, working with circular motions. Use droplets of mineral oil to lubricate the tampon as necessary. As you progress and the shellac film becomes thicker and smoother, a pleasing cloud will appear on the surface. This is caused by the lubricant.

Build up the film of shellac in three or four installments with a night's drying time between each. When the desired thickness and smoothness is reached, eliminate the oil from the surface. With a new, clean tampon and alcohol alone, wipe off the oil, following the grain of the wood, and unveil in all its splendor a clean, transparent finish. Remember, true French polishing is more than a skill, it is almost an art, and like most arts, cannot be learned only from books.

---

applications can be a little heavier, but you must not rush. You will need a certain amount of skill and a great deal of patience. You could also try two coats of a dilute, lukewarm solution of bleached hide glue, well sanded, under any clear finish.

I'm making a large roll-top bread box. My problem is finding a sealer for the wood that won't retain an odor, so it doesn't contaminate my breads.

Buy a good brand of shellac, white for light wood, orange for dark. Make sure it is fresh and keep it in a glass container. Cut it one measure of shellac to three of alcohol, and apply two or three even coats with a soft brush. Let each coat dry thoroughly and sandpaper with fine grit between coats. When the third coat is dry, cut the finish with 4/0 or 5/0 steel wool—rub until it is very smooth to the touch. Then apply a thin coat of paste wax, let dry and rub clean with an old wool sock. The secret is to use very little finishing material and a lot of rubbing and sanding.

Open-pore French polishing, another way to French polish, was practiced widely in the first twenty years of this century. This is a good way to retain the natural color of wood. Here is how to do it.

First, sand the wood impeccably smooth, then brush or blow the dust off, leaving the pores open. With the tampon, apply thin films of shellac as before, except this time work with the direction of the grain. No pumice is used, no attempt is made to fill the pores, and no oil is used in open-pore French polishing. The tampon should never be too moist, and each film must be allowed to dry before the next is applied. This type of French polishing does not have the bright, glossy shine of the filled version, but it is far easier to obtain and still quite pleasant to regard.

Lacquer—Today, lacquer finishes are the best. They offer excellent protection to the wood, and if they are properly applied, enhance its natural beauty. Moreover, lacquers are versatile, and there is a special kind for nearly every need.

The problem is that most lacquers must be sprayed. To work with them one needs compressed air and a spray gun. Spraying lacquer creates a fire hazard and charges the air with noxious fumes; to cope with these problems, factories build special rooms with huge exhaust fans, but for the home craftsman the difficulties are hard to overcome.

There are four things to consider in setting up a lacquer-spraying system in the shop: the spray gun, the object to spray, the baffle and the exhaust fan. The gun, aimed at the object, will determine the location of the fan, but if the fan is directly in line with the direction of spray it will divert air flow and much of the finishing material will land on the blades of its propeller. That is why you need a baffle placed directly behind the object. The air and the finishing material will hit the object and the excess will be deflected by the baffle. The exhaust should be placed behind and above the baffle's upper half.

Baffle   Exhaust fan

Gun

The usual lacquer finish consists of one coat of sanding sealer (a variety of lacquer modified for easy sanding) followed by three or four coats of lacquer. Of course, before finishing, your wood has to be perfectly sandpapered and dust-free. Each coat of lacquer, whether applied by spraying or by brushing, must be thoroughly dry and sandpapered again with finer and finer grits before you apply the next coat. Some people use as many as ten to fifteen coats of lacquer. The last rubbing should be done with either the finest steel wool you can find, or with water and pumice (see my discussion of rubbing out a lacquer finish on page 70). You may, if you choose, follow this up with a light waxing, polished up with wool.

You can also use lacquer to fill the pores of the wood (as discussed on page 52). In addition, there are on the market some brands of so-called padding lacquers, to be applied somewhat like French polish. If you can get some, experiment with it.

Many woodworkers have asked me what Chinese lacquer is and how to apply it. Scant is the information available concerning Oriental lacquer. The Hindustani word *lakh* refers to a product of the *Laccifer lacca* insect. When refined, the gummy deposit of these insects produces shellac and resin-lac, the main ingredient in the process called japaning. Chinese lacquer, however, is not produced by insects. It starts with the juices of the lac-tree *(Rhus vernicifera)*, which is related to the American sumac tree. The thick, milklike sap is collected during the summer months from trees that are at least ten years old, and when dehydrated and purified becomes the base of Oriental lacquer. It very well could be that the process of refining the sap and making it into lacquer was a closely guarded secret, but I have my doubts about that. It is more probable that no Westerner learned or recorded the process properly.

Chinese lacquering is not a true wood-finishing process, as it obliterates the color and the markings of the wood. The study of Chinese lacquer, however, does interest wood finishers, for the possible adaptation of this marvelous sap to our needs. The smoothness of the most beautifully French-polished object is easily matched by the porcelainlike finish of Chinese lacquer, and even if we assume both to be equal in smoothness, the lacquer will offer unquestionably greater protection to the wood. Let me illustrate. When archeologists excavated the Lo-lang tombs in Japan (many of which had been flooded for several centuries) they found lacquered objects floating—un-harmed—in the water. Likewise, nearly two years after a ship carrying a Japanese exhibit from Vienna sank, divers recovered lacquered ob-jects from the wreck—undamaged. Chinese lacquer actually hardens when exposed to water, and is also resistant to acids, heat and shock. It has an enemy, however, and that is bright light. Exposed to bright light, Chinese lacquer will fade, dry out and eventually decompose.

The application of Chinese lacquer approximates our own lacquer-ing techniques. First the wood is filled (using mostly starches such as powdered rice combined with the sap from the smaller branches of the lac-tree). With infinite care and patience, the wood is filled and refilled, then undercoated with many layers of a sap called *seshime*. Only when the wood is as smooth as the caress of a summer breeze does the actual lacquering start. Thirty to forty coats of lacquer are spread on the object, and each coat is patiently sanded down with whetstones and volcanic ashes (similar to pumice). Later on, these are replaced with a type of clay (similar to rottenstone). The final rubbing is completed with charred deer antler, followed by pine soot.

Varnish—Oils combined through a complicated process with chemi-cals, resins and plasticizers (called solids) are no longer oils but var-nishes. Varnish was not born yesterday—both the ancient Greeks and Egyptians knew about it, but from the days of the pharaohs up to the twentieth century, varnish did not improve as much as it has dur-ing the last fifty years. While only a half century ago the best varnish took twenty-four hours to dry and twenty-four hours more before it could be rubbed out, there are varnishes on the market today that will dry within an hour and can be rubbed out in four hours. The woodworking industry prefers lacquer to varnish because of still faster drying time, but for the small shop without spraying equip-ment, modern varnishes are a blessing.

On the shelves of your corner paint store are the world's best var-nishes in all varieties. Simple horse sense will tell you which to choose—phenolic varnish, polyurethane varnish, alkyd resin var-nish, to name a few. More expensive ingredients are involved in mak-ing a marine (phenolic) varnish, for example, than in making the var-nish you would use on interior trim. Read the labels to find the best varnish for the job and how to use it. There are a number of books on the market that deal with varnishes, but they mostly state facts that are self-evident. Varnish should be applied in a clean, dust-free room with clean brushes. If you would follow the instructions on the can to the letter, fill the wood with the right filler, prime it with the right primer (if one is called for), and apply the right number of varnish coats with proper sanding in between, you would achieve a measurable thickness of rugged film on your wood. Although manufacturers are often against using finishes such as Varathane over

Questions about varnish

I make music boxes of walnut and clocks of cherry, oak and walnut. I have had satisfactory results with polyurethane finish. I was asked by a customer to make a music box of rosewood, and then I ran into trouble. Any urethane finish that I attempted to use failed to cure properly. I finally settled on Deft clear wood finish. This finish dries rapidly, but it is not as hard as urethane. Can you help me?

The oils in rosewood are not compatible with finishing products, so first you must rid your wood of its oil. Wash the rosewood generously with gasoline, being sure to ventilate your work area well and to avoid contact with sparks or fire. Let dry. Apply a coat of fresh orange shellac cut fifty percent with alcohol. Let dry. Sandpaper, and you can safely continue with your urethane. It will dry to your satisfaction.

I glued 1/40-inch rosewood veneer to a base, sanded it smooth, then filled it with an appropriate-colored filler. I let the filler dry, sanded it smooth, then sprayed on Varathane satin finish. The problem is, it wouldn't dry, remaining tacky over most of the area, especially the darkest area. Next I tried a sample as follows: sanded, cleaned with alcohol, sanded again, filled, sprayed. Some areas were still tacky. What's the problem?

Your problem—I guess—is the sequence of finishing products that you used. The culprit is probably the filler. The remedy with the greatest chance of success is this: Wipe off the present finish with a rag soaked in gasoline. Let dry, repeat once more. If the tackiness is gone, you are on the right track. Spray on the wood a thin coat of fresh orange shellac, using lots of air and little shellac, so it dries practically as you spray. Let dry overnight and repeat, this time a bit heavier. The two coats of shellac should seal the finish already

lacquer, it can be done and in some cases is the right thing to do. You can avoid problems if you seal your sanding-sealer base with a good coat of lacquer and let it dry thoroughly. After light sanding, spray the Varathane in extremely light coats so each will dry quickly. This way, the two finishes will not melt and mix.

The film that a coat of oil leaves on the wood after curing is almost immeasurably thin, but three coats of varnish, properly applied, will leave on the wood about $\frac{1}{64}$ inch of film. In this respect, there is a

on the wood. After proper drying and light sanding, discontinue Varathane and use a good grade of spar varnish (such as McCloskey's Spar Varnish—a phenolic alkyd resin varnish) as recommended by the manufacturer.

If wiping with gasoline does not remedy the tackiness, I am afraid you will have to wash the present finish off and start again. If such is the case, since you have a spray outfit, alcohol-proof lacquer is your best bet, used as per manufacturer's directions.

I have recently purchased an old house in which the den walls are covered with cypress. It appears as if the walls were originally sealed with a thin coat of clear varnish. Where pictures have hung, the wood is lighter in color than the remaining walls, which have darkened through exposure. How might I blend these lighter spots into the remaining wall?

There is no simple answer, although someone specializing in photographic chemistry might be able to help you. My approach would be the French one: *aux grands maux les grands remèdes* (for big problems, strong remedies). I would take the panels off the walls and run them through the planer, taking off $\frac{1}{64}$ inch. Then sandpaper them and put them back. In the long run this may be easier than working with chemicals toward a very uncertain solution. Good luck.

What is the best technique for preventing the deterioration of varnish, etc., in partially empty cans?

It may not be the best technique, but my way of doing it is this. I reseal the partially empty can as tightly as possible and store it upside down until I need it again.

great similarity between varnish and lacquer finishes. Both need filling and multiple coats, and both end up as measurable transparent
films, although in general varnish films have a golden hue and lacquer films are almost colorless. A light rubbing with 4/0 steel wool
along with a light application of paste wax shined up with a wool rag
will yield a pleasant finish. This finish, however, will not satisfy the
perfectionist who is intent on achieving a mirrorlike surface. The
built-up finish is seemingly smooth, but only *seemingly*. The perfectionist will want to return to mechanical methods for rubbing out the
finish—using pumice and rottenstone.

Abrasives for Rubbing Out the Finish

In the first act of our finishing play we made the wood smooth via
mechanical means, including sandpaper and filler. In the second act
we coated the wood with various film-forming products. Now, in the
third and last act, we return to mechanical means to rub out built-up
finishes (oil and wax finishes are rubbed out as they are applied) in
order to bring about the ultimate smoothness of the wood.

As a rule, the quality of a finish equals the degree of its smoothness.
To achieve superior smoothness, superior abrasives are needed. A re-
view of these must start with steel wool, favored by many for the final
rubbing. My opinion of steel wool is that it is extremely useful as a
cleaning tool. A coarse grade is a great help in removing old finishes
from the wood, and I use a finer grade to clean off filler. As a final
abrasive, however, steel wool is overrated, though it can come in
handy when working on finishes where, for reasons of economy, two
or three coats of finish are heaped on the wood with not much sanding in between. In this case, 4/0 steel wool will cut the finish to a silky
appearance, making the haphazard acceptable. In America, soap
pads combining soap with steel wool are commonplace. Similar pads,
where the steel wool is coated with wax, are used in furniture factories—in one operation the furniture is both rubbed and waxed.
Soon such pads will probably be available to craftsmen who are in a
hurry. Since I never am, I will not buy them. At this stage of finish-

ing, when we are looking for a superior finish, we must turn away from steel wool and turn to fine, powdered abrasives.

Abrasives are an integral part of modern life. On my humble storage shelf there are at least half a dozen abrasives unknown to the average wood finisher. Many of these are micrograded. I cannot explain how micrograding works, but it seems to me that the 220 aluminum oxide is coarser than the 275 is. Compared to them, the 80 silicon carbide seems terribly coarse, while the 10W7 garnet is velvety smooth. The difference among the 85 barnesite, the Grox cerium oxide and the 25 red rouge is way beyond my ability to evaluate. The only reason I mention them is to show that modern technology produces hundreds of abrasive grades but we poor, backward wood finishers steadfastly hold onto the two used by our forefathers—pumice and rottenstone.

Now, nothing is wrong with these. Pumice, a hard, volcanic stone, is marketed in four grades. In the earliest stages of rubbing, 2F is adequate; in the latest stages 4F, the finest grade, is too coarse. A lubricant is needed with pumice, and while many good finishers select clean mineral oil cut with ten percent to twenty percent mineral spirits, I prefer rainwater into which I throw, as they become available, the salvaged remains of soap bars.

While the pumice cuts the finish film fairly quickly, eliminating some imperfections, at a certain point it must give way to a still finer abrasive, rottenstone. Rottenstone must be used with water as a lubricant (the rainwater/soap combination is best) because oil will always leave a microscopic film on the finish. Properly used, rottenstone will bring out a glossy, mirrorlike smoothness, the ultimate improvement of the tactile quality of wood.

The tools used to apply these abrasives are simple, almost primitive. For some wood finishers, a pad made of rags will do; others use a three-inch by five-inch block with a ¼-inch felt pad glued to the bottom. Still others replace the felt with leather and swear that donkey hide is best. In France we used leather alone. We took a two-inch to three-inch wide belt or hide, rolled it tightly until this buffer was about four inches in diameter, and tied it with string. Then we made one side flat on sandpaper and carved the other side to fit comfortably into our palms. We kept this tool in paraffin oil.

Now there are electric tools available to speed up and ease the task.

I have had success with orbital and reciprocating sanders, using them with a felt pad on the bottom and water to polish the finish with rottenstone. The wool cap, adapted to the common electric drill, acts like a mechanical towel and is useful for final buffing. I would not use any machine on, say, a jewelry box, but if I had ten desks to rub out I would be loath to use anything else.

Rubbing Out the Finish

I will now summarize the steps involved in bringing a surface to mirror smoothness. I will use a lacquer finish for an example, but the techniques are almost the same for varnish.

Generally speaking, lacquering can be divided into four operations: filling the pores, sealing, coating with the lacquer and, finally, rubbing out. The filler, with rare exceptions, is the same as the one that would be used under varnish and it should be applied exactly the same way. Remember that the filler should remain nowhere but in the pores of the wood, and make sure that the color of the filler matches the color of the wood. After all excess filler has been cleaned off, apply the sanding sealer. A well-filled wood, properly coated with sealer and sanded with 150-grit to 200-grit paper, is well on its way to acquiring the smoothness desired.

The average finisher follows up these operations with three, sometimes four, coatings of clear gloss lacquer, sanding between coats with finer and finer grits. By the time the fourth coat is ready to be applied, the wood is perfectly smooth and the pores are practically unnoticeable. This is the moment of truth. The surface may be satisfactory to most finishers, but for the exacting finisher it will fall short. At this stage, the finisher must decide whether he or she wants a rubbed finish, entailing much more work, or an easier one. If the finisher opts for the latter, the last coat of lacquer should be either flat (dull) or semi-flat lacquer. Either of these, when dry, will dress up the finish with a dull or semi-dull shine.

More exacting finishers strive for the best. Without any hesitation we spray the last coat of lacquer on the wood, but lo and behold, we spray on the same clear gloss lacquer we have been using all along. This may be the last coat (although some finishers use as many as ten to fifteen coats), but the job is not finished yet. Now the rub comes in. The surface is smooth, we agree on that, but it is not as smooth as a mirror, because, in spite of all caution and care, the spray carries minute particles of dust with it. Rubbing out will level off these micromountains of dust.

Decide whether you want a glossy finish or a discreet satiny shine. The road to the first goes through the second. The finest sandpaper is far too rough to use at this point, so we must use pumice stone (4F is good), applying it with a cloth or felt pad. Keep this pad impeccably clean at all times. Sprinkle the pumice on the wood and with the pad, rub it in the direction of the grain using water or mineral oil cut three to one with mineral spirits. Few are not satisfied with such a satin finish. If the glossy mirror finish is your goal, however, you must clean off all traces of pumice, and with a new pad, repeat the process with rottenstone, using water as a lubricant. A few more ingredients are required at this point: energy, care, patience and skill, but with the combination of all these you can achieve the best possible finish in the world.

On the Unfinished Finish

Throughout this chapter I have stated that the smoother the wood, the better the finish. Now I state that there are exceptions to this rule. Such an exception was the job I did for James J. Rorimer, the prestigious director of the Metropolitan Museum of Art in New York City during the early 1960s. He commissioned me to build five huge doors and a series of shutters for the Blumenthal Spanish Pavilion of the museum. When you worked for a person like Rorimer, you didn't talk, you listened. He explained every detail of the job to me and, in fact, the plans and specifications were so detailed and strict I needed no imagination or initiative. I carried out Rorimer's instructions to the letter, and the job was ready for finishing.

At this point the specifications ordered: 1) Use no mechanical tools such as planes, scrapers or sanders; 2) use only hand-activated roughing planes, the markings of which must remain clearly visible; 3) use no sandpaper of any kind; 4) use no stain, dye or finish of any kind on the surface. Rorimer wanted those doors (exposed to heavy traffic not too far from the main entrance of the museum) completely naked and unprotected. My pleading with him to let me use some wax nearly brought about an abrupt end to our friendly relationship.

Today the doors are still there and while one may say they are dirty, others may say they are aged and enhanced by a precious patina. Rorimer died in 1966, and now I can admit that I tricked him. I did not put any finishing material on the doors, and yet I finished them just the same. How? With chain cloth salvaged from a medieval suit of armor and with much elbow grease, I rubbed and burnished the naked wood until it acquired a discreet glow. Rorimer noticed it, ran his hand over the rough yet smooth wood and rewarded me with an approving smile.

There are no rules or regulations, no rhyme or reason in the use of rough lumber. Out of old weather-beaten barn sides clever decorators create beautiful paneling. Some plywood is manufactured from roughsawn lumber—obviously because people are buying it. Making the most heteroclite objects out of driftwood is an industry of its own. Handhewn posts and beams are found in some of the most sophisticated interiors.

What does finishing have to do with these ragged, coarse, craggy woods? The weather-beaten barn sides and driftwood have been finished by a master finisher—Mother Nature. She can produce colors, bleaches, shadings and harmonies that no human can ever hope to duplicate, but nevertheless we may get ideas and inspiration from her.

Accentuating the
Markings of the Wood

Chapter Five

Late in the nineteenth and early in the twentieth century in central Europe, occasional attempts were made to fill the pores of the wood decoratively. My professor at the Technological Institute of Budapest mentioned it as a distinct possibility and as a fact in finishing history—wood can be dyed one color and its pores filled with another color. This was all I knew about the process when I decided to experiment. I will not bore you with the tales of the number of samples I burned in the fireplace of my villa, but instead I will simply tell you of my success.

First I procured almost a hundred sample-sized boards, two-thirds of them quartersawn and flatsawn oak selected for the grain, and the remainder ash and chestnut. All samples were about ¼ inch thick and measured six inches by ten inches, close to the "Golden Section," developed in ancient Greece, which says that in a perfect rectangle, the relationship between the short and long sides should be the same as the relationship between the long side and the sum of a long and short side. I sanded all the samples to perfection on both sides and all edges. My goal was to make two identical sets of samples, each set containing fifteen boards.

The second operation was dyeing. Of the final samples in each set, the backgrounds of four were jet black, four more were close to chocolate brown, and four more were a beautiful red. There was one blue, one green and one purple sample among each set. The techniques I used to dye the samples are discussed in chapter two. My primary coloring ingredients were logwood, yellow-wood and Brazil-wood extracts. The colors I produced were deep and clear. The red was like a cardinal's cape and the black, when you visit the Carlsbad

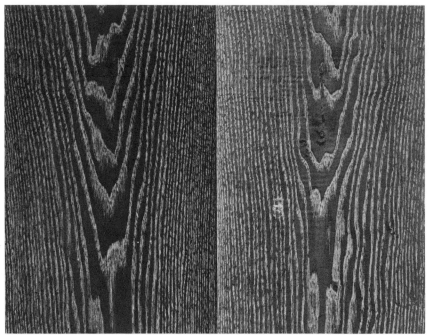

The wood in the board at left is oak dyed maroon with an off white filler. In the board at right, the oak is dyed medium blue and has a light blue filler.

A commercial application of the decorative pore-filling process, used on a milk bar in Paris.

Caverns and near the center of the earth and the guide turns off all the lights to show you what *total* darkness is...my black was a little darker yet. The wood looked as though the given color was its natural one, and every marking was clearly discernible. The key to such colors is as much in the preparation of the dye as in the constant fine sanding, but before, during and after each operation I sanded my samples, so there would be no problem of the grain raising ever.

Before sealing in my beautiful colors, I got rid of all the dust both on the wood and in the pores. In France one can find an unsurpassed variety of brushes; the kind I used for this application was made of wire, but it was not the kind of wire brush we are accustomed to here. This brush measured about two inches by five inches and had wires less than one inch long. The wires looked like brass yet were springy like steel, and the thickness of each was not much more than that of a human hair. With such a brush, followed by brushing with a soft hair brush, I cleaned away all the dust. Only when this was done did I seal in the colors.

I began with a nearly dry pad that left on the wood with every pass a mere breath of white shellac thinned with alcohol. I heaped on the wood a few hundred layers of shellac, but this film measured only about $\frac{1}{100}$th of the thickness of a cigarette paper, and the pores remained clean, clear and empty. I let the wood dry overnight and continued the next day and the day after that.

On the fourth day I was ready for the filler. The only filler that I know will fill all the pores fully is plaster of paris. Plaster of paris is available in several grades, the finest being the molding grade used by dentists and sculptors. This grade is the one that I used. The fast drying time of plaster of paris can be retarded somewhat by the addition of lime, and its hardness can be tempered with simple whiting powder. The composition of my filler was seventy-five percent plaster, twenty percent whiting and five percent lime. To this mixture I then added dry colors.

What color filler should be used on which background? At least half my samples were filled with a much lighter shade of the background color—light gray in black, beige in brown. For a striking effect, I put a sharp medium green filler in a black sample, a lemon yellow filler in black, white in black, white in red and yellow in brown.

Now everybody knows that plaster must be mixed with water be-

Drafting board and work cabinet designed by Paul M. Finelli. The wood is wormy chestnut dyed dark brown, the filler is beige.

The wood of this breakfront is wormy chestnut. Frank and his men applied a coat of clear lacquer to the wood, then painted it with thinned-down asphaltum paint to darken the pores. The wood was then cleaned off, and a second coat of lacquer applied.

fore it is applied, and everybody knows that once mixed, plaster hardens within minutes, even when lime and whiting are used with it. To get around wasting a great deal of plaster, I mixed only as much filler as I could use up in two or three minutes. This filler I pressed hard into the pores of the wood with rotating motions of my fingers. I wiped off the excess with rags after checking every pore, leaving a fraction more filler than needed rather than less. Cleaning off the excess filler was the hardest part of the job. I used the finest grade of sandpaper, care and patience. The wood was protected by a fine film of shellac, and I had to take off the excess filler without damaging this film. The effect of my samples was now striking, but still far from my goal, so I French polished the surface of the wood.

About two weeks later I had my two sets of samples in all of their splendor. Behind the mirrorlike surface was wood with interesting markings and color, and on this color each and every pore was clearly marked with a distinct second color. Each sample was protected by a sheet of gray felt and a neat cardboard cover. People looking at them had the feeling that they were handling something rare and precious. These were the samples that got me the coveted job at Jansen's working with Fernand Naveilhan.

The Blue Dining-Room Set

In the late 1920s, the star of the house of Jansen was rising. The three directors felt that the company should open a new branch catering to modern tastes and styles, and to my surprise gave me 30,000 francs to open up the cabinetmaking shop of Frank and Co., 5 Passage Saint Bernard, Paris. Frank is myself, the company was Jansen, and Passage Saint Bernard is at the very center of the Faubourg Saint Antoine, the woodworking hub of Paris. I had just turned twenty-five.

I designed, manufactured and finished a few occasional pieces, tables, bars and hanging cabinets and at the same time built my *chef d'oeuvre*, an Art-Deco-style dining-room set fit for a king. The wood was oak, the grain precisely selected, matched and painstakingly fitted in repeated patterns on every piece. The hardware was silver-plated, the glass and mirrors beveled. The set was dyed jet black and each and every pore was filled with pure ultramarine blue. I French polished the set and too late realized its staggering cost—half of my working capital and no buyer—not even a prospect of one—in sight. My bank balance was alarmingly low, and I decided I had better turn to my benefactors for help.

This was a month after the New York stock market had collapsed, and the directors of Jansen listened to my story without any sign of sympathy. Soon afterward I learned Jansen's reply: no additional loans. Furthermore, I would have to choose between bankruptcy (selling the shop and all its assets) or buying Jansen's interest in the shop, which entailed the signing of 30,000 francs' worth of notes to be paid, with interest, within five years. I signed the notes and before the end of the year Frank and Co. ceased to exist. Now I owned my own company.

I was paralyzed by the lack of money, but one day my luck changed. Alone, brooding over the hopelessness of my situation, I was sweeping the last shavings from the floor when someone walked into my shop. "My name is Alatsas and I have a cabinet shop in the next block," said the man. "I have problems with finishing and thought you could help me out." An hour later a truckload of freshly manufactured pieces was unloaded, and two hours later I was in the midst of finishing them. Alatsas provided me with as much work as I could handle and paid me honestly besides. In a few weeks I had to hire a helper, a second one, then a third. Things began to look up.

In the meantime, my beautiful blue-black dining-room set, covered with blankets, used up much-needed space in my small shop. Now came the second part of the miracle. On the Grand Boulevard in the heart of Paris a store became vacant. Soon, my dining-room set was in the most conspicuous window in Paris, with a sign proclaiming that it was finished by George Frank, master finisher. My fifteen samples were placed prominently in the foreground. Two weeks later, my helpers and I started finishing the woodwork of a large movie theater, all in black oak filled with white, my first large-scale commercial work using decorative pore-filling.

We did not finish the theater before receiving another big contract, finishing the interior of a large fur salon in Paris. The color combination there was quite unusual—a light gray-brown background filled with red. The working method on both jobs was the same. At the time, early in 1930, most woodworking shops did their own veneering. The glue used, mostly warm hide glue, frequently invaded the pores of the thin veneers. I soon realized that I could not put filler in pores that were already filled, and therefore my first task was to clean the pores. I soaked the wood in lukewarm water, then wiped off all excess and wire-brushed the moist wood with a rotating motion. This soaking did not loosen the veneer except in the rare spots where it was improperly glued. The wire brush I used—indispensable in my shops—was approximately 2½ inches wide and seven inches long with 1¾-inch fine wire strands. This brush could reach into the pores of the wood and kick out all debris, and was a major factor in the success of the decorative pore-filling process. New, clean, sharp brushes do a better job than tired, dull ones.

Dyeing the wood, always preceded by sandpapering, was next. By this time I had no more use for old-fashioned dyes. Arti A.G. provided me with dyes requiring no guesswork. Sealing the dyed wood was done the old way, by padding on white shellac.

In addition to the use of commercial dye, there was another step in the commercialization of the decorative pore-filling process. We replaced the plaster with a filler easier to work with—pure whiting powder and bleached wax, which came in four-inch discs about ¼ inch thick. To about two pounds of whiting I added a half pound of melted bleached wax to which had been added enough mineral spirits to give the wax the consistency of heavy cream. This filler was easy to rub into the pores and easy to wipe off. The wax, when the spirits evaporated, acted as a binder. Dry colors could add any hue of the rainbow. Then, leaving the pores about eighty percent filled, we finished the wood with the open-pore method of French polishing, which I discuss on page 63.

This simple filler filled not only the pores of square miles of wood, it also helped to fill my very empty coffers—I paid off two years ahead of time the last installment of my debt. This was made possible by yet another miracle. I sold the blue dining-room set to a textile merchant of Roubaix, a town near the Belgian border.

The last step in the commercialization of the decorative pore-filling process was not filling the pores at all. Let us assume the wood is dyed black. It is sealed, all pores are open and clean, awaiting the filler.

The pecky cypress on these walls and the ceiling has been finished with céruse, a thin white paint. After the wood is sealed, the paint is applied, then wiped off the background with rags. The paint remains in the pores, producing an effect similar to that of white filler.

Now, instead of filler, you could paint the wood with a thinned-down paint and clean off the black background (protected by the shellac seal) with rags, leaving the paint in the pores. The paint will not fill them, but it will color them white, producing practically the same effect as white filler. *Céruse*, both in English and French, is the name of a heavy-bodied white paint. Thinned *céruse* was frequently used for this fake filling, so frequently, in fact, that the French name for the whole process is *céruser*.

A last word about cleaning the pores: Glue and dirt obstruct the pores, but never fill them fully. There is always room for the filler, so a second consideration: Thoroughly cleaned pores took too much filler and assumed an unwanted dominance. Other finishers, who filled their wood without wire-brushing, often achieved a less striking effect than we did, yet I must admit, the result was more subdued and more discreet.

If you think we have exhausted the possibilities this technique offers, think again. Imagine that you start with a wood you want to dye red. Somewhere you make a mistake and it turns out a nondescript gray-black-reddish color, exactly what you don't want. The wood has excellent figure, so you spray a good, heavy coat of red-tinted lacquer on it, covering up your botched dye job, and then you fill or simply tint the pores with your selected color—any of the rainbow's. You will not be too far from your planned color scheme. You canceled out most of the readability of the wood, but its figure will still sing out loud and clear.

The choices are up to you. I know of no other means of finishing that provides all the possibilities of this method. There are, however, other methods of accentuating the markings of the wood. One of them is scorching the wood, as the next tale describes.

The Charred Bedroom Suite

I should have known better than to accept an invitation to lunch from Maurice Lafaille, the interior decorator who had presented me with the task of producing the color of virgin hemp on wood. Sure

The result of Frank's experimentation: before scorching, edge; after scorching, top.

enough, when the main dish was served, Lafaille produced a small package about six inches square. At his request I opened it and unveiled a finely detailed statuette of Buddha. He asked me what I thought of it, and I answered that it seemed to be exquisitely carved, a work of art without any doubt, but that I was far from being a competent judge of its value. "George, take a closer look at the hair," he said, and I did. The hair was made of fine lines, each about the thickness of a human hair, but the color of the lines alternated, light and dark, light and dark. Lafaille then gave me a powerful magnifying glass. I saw that the dark lines were produced by fire or burning and the light ones were the natural color of the wood. How the wood was scorched in such narrow bands was a mystery to me.

"And what do you think of it now?" inquired Lafaille. "Simple," I replied. "If I did not have this thing in my hand, I would say that such a job is impossible." Lafaille then dropped the bombshell. "George, I am designing a bedroom suite for the Baron Rotschild, and this is the finish you are going to do for me."

I called him an idiot and an imbecile and told him that, even if I could do the finish, it would take me at least 200 years. "George, you do it," said Lafaille. He paid for lunch and we hurried to my shop.

Lafaille was right; he knew me well. The problem did not let me sleep. The next day I borrowed my girlfriend's electric iron, my elderly neighbor's charcoal iron, several soldering irons—and got nowhere. I cursed Lafaille, but I kept looking for the solution. I spilled alcohol on the wood and set it afire, then tried slower-burning turpentine with the same results: zero.

There must be a special god helping wood finishers. A lead pipe, carrying water to my kitchen, sprung a leak. I called a plumber, who fixed the leak with a blowtorch. This gave me an idea. The next day I had my own blowtorch and as I scorched the surface of my sample fir board, I knew I was on the right track. With a stiff brush I could easily take off the completely charred soft part of the wood grain (the earlywood layer of each year's growth) and uncover light, uncharred wood beneath. The hard veins (the latewood) remained dark, scorched, intact. With each experiment I came closer to the solution, and the next day Lafaille took my samples to the Baron. He was thrilled. He sent his Rolls Royce to fetch us, and that day I learned the true meaning of haute cuisine.

Floor space at the Foire de Paris (Paris trade show) was costly, but wall space was virtually free. Here George Frank displayed his samples, top. He remembers, 'The woodworking trade did not take long to notice me.' This notice enabled Frank to set up a booth at the 1936 fair, above. The two chairs in the foreground are shown after and before bleaching; the fifteen samples hang on the wall.

About two months later the Baron's bedroom suite was ready to be scorch-finished. Both the Baron and Lafaille came to the shop to watch me char the surface of the wood. If there is a god helping wood finishers, there must be gremlins who make innovators' lives miserable. The intense heat of the blowtorch made the wood shrink, crack, split and bend before our very eyes. In less than half an hour the bedroom suite was ruined, or at least the parts I burned with my blowtorch were. Tears ran from my eyes, not only from the smoke, but from the realization that I had failed.

Without any doubt, the scorched finish was something new, original and beautiful, and neither Lafaille nor I was ready to throw in the towel. We decided that the bedroom suite had to be rebuilt, but that the wood must be burned before furniture was made of it. Moreover, we adopted a frame-and-panel construction to allow further shrinkage. The Baron agreed and assured us that he would assume the cost regardless of how many times I had to rebuild his furniture. Two or three months later, we delivered the first bedroom suite made of scorched pine to the Baron Rotschild's country home at Chantilly. It may still be there today.

Sandblasting

My narrow escape from bankruptcy in 1929 taught me my lesson well. The first duty of a boss is to sell. The experience of my odd dining-room set displayed in the very center of Paris brought home the second truth. It pays to advertise. The *Foire de Paris* (Paris trade show) took place annually, but the prices of the booths rented to tradesmen were way beyond my reach. The abundant wall space, however, was unused, unwanted and unsold, and I could rent acres of it for very little money. Every year I exhibited my samples there, and the woodworking trade did not take long to notice me.

Finishing was then, as it is now, the problem child of the woodworking industry. The calls for my help were frequent, and soon the better half of my income was derived from the fees I collected from troubled furniture manufacturers all over western Europe.

A storefront in Paris, about 1933, of sandblasted spruce with dark highlights.

The address of my shop became well known in woodworking circles and among interior decorators, but soon I realized that my shop was not the only attraction on the street. Omer Rapseat rented the space next door to me. Rapseat was a talented sculptor who specialized in carving glass. How does one carve glass? I had not the faintest idea until I saw him doing it with sand and compressed air.

Rapseat's assistant, André, sandblasted my first samples with disastrous results. The sand dug deep into the wood in some spots and hardly at all in others. I had the feeling I could have done better myself, and I told Rapseat as much. The next set of samples was handled by the master himself. A new way of emphasizing the natural grain of the wood was revealed to me.

For those not familiar with sandblasting, here is a short description. Compressed air propels the sand with great force against the object to be blasted (usually made out of stone or brick, as sandblasting is used primarily to clean old buildings). The stream of sand can be controlled, as can the air pressure, but the person working the jet must always be careful to achieve the same degree of roughness, moderate to heavy, over the entire surface of the object.

Many times in the sandblasting trade large areas of an object must be protected from the ravages of the sand. Rapseat had several ways to do this. He had a soft, reusable, rubbery tape that resisted the strongest blasts, and he also developed his own protective gel. Its main ingredient was the same hide glue woodworkers use, to which was added an oily substance, probably glycerine, to keep the gel from hardening through. With fine instruments, Rapseat could cut away the shape to be sandblasted while safeguarding the rest of the object.

Two bedrooms—Sandblasting is the finish I used on the bedroom set of the Pasha of Marrakesh. The set was made of English quartersawn oak; the veneer was sawn lumber, about $\frac{1}{8}$ inch to $\frac{3}{16}$ inch thick, safely glued to a lumber core. The lines of the set were the simplest possible. Rapseat himself did the sandblasting—anything less than perfection would have been rejected.

After sandblasting, I dyed the wood black, sealed it by brushing on a few coats of black-tinted shellac, and then French polished until I obtained brilliant highlights on the rugged surface—an interesting contrast. Under these highlights were the matte areas of the much-

The bedroom suite of the Pasha of Marrakesh, finished by Frank with sandblasting and black dye, was featured in one of France's leading interior-decoration magazines. This dressing table is a piece from that set.

enlarged pores; the effect was quite pleasing. Jean Pascaud, a top decorator in Paris who had commissioned me to do the job, was legitimately proud of the bedroom set. He received well-deserved acclaim
and free publicity when the Pasha's bedroom became the subject of
an article in France's leading trade magazine. Too late did he realize
that the article gave away the secret of sandblasting.

By this time, a second bedroom suite that Pascaud had commissioned me to finish was ready. Pascaud imposed the greatest secrecy
and would not reveal the identity of the customer. He hinted,
however, that the customer was an abdicated king, and that he was
offering the bedroom suite as a gift to his wife, an American.

The wood was quartersawn oak with grain as straight as grain
could be. Earlier I stressed how I abhor peroxide bleaching, yet after
sandblasting we bleached this set until it was the color of platinum-
blond hair. It lost all its original coloring, but because of the beautiful
vertical grain this did not matter. The end result was a raindroplike
quality, exactly what I had wanted. Then we applied a few coats of
shellac, pigmented slightly with white enamel, and polished up the
protruding areas to the utmost smoothness. The set was already fit
for a queen, yet I had a few more tricks up my sleeve.

Artists use a crystal-clear varnish on their paintings for protection.
This varnish can be thinned down to a watery consistency with
turpentine. Some artists apply this varnish with a brush; others prefer a mouth blower, an instrument consisting of two thin metal tubes
angled at ninety degrees. With the pressure of your lungs, the varnish
will shoot out and cover the painting.

I bought a few ounces of varnish, thinned it down with turpentine
and blew the mixture lightly over the bedroom suite, but not before I
had mixed in some finely ground aluminum powder. Then I cleaned
the protruding areas first with rags moistened with turpentine, then
with dry rags, leaving traces of silver in the deep areas—not enough
to show, but enough to reflect the light here and there.

The last innovation was the revival of an old trick—the
trompe-l'oeil. Looking at the bureau from the front, you could see half
of a long black glove hanging out of the top drawer, loose change and
paper money scattered on the top, as well as the stubs of two opera
tickets and a half-opened lacy fan. You had to come within a yard of
the bureau to discern that there was no glove hanging out of the

drawer and nothing on top. They had been painted on by an artist who could trick *(trompe)* the eye *(l'oeil)*. These areas, of course, had not been sandblasted.

Unfortunately, because of the secrecy of this project (the bedroom suite was always covered, in the shop and in transit) there was never any possibility of taking pictures.

Sandblasted Carvings

Monsieur Mariage ran the biggest furniture factory in France and by the end of 1933 was shipping 150 to 200 bedroom and dining-room sets per day. This was when I first met him. He came to my stand at the Paris fair and said, "I have problems with finishing. Could you come to my factory outside of Paris and help me?" "Yes, I can," I replied. "What is your fee, then?" I did some fast thinking. Although Jansen had paid me 12,000 francs for a year, I blurted out "10,000 francs for two weeks." Without batting an eye Mariage said, "Come as soon as you can."

In Monsieur Mariage's factory, flatbed conveyor cars moved on tracks much like a railroad. The pieces to be finished were loaded on the cars, which moved a little faster than a foot per minute. About a hundred workers, mostly unskilled women, were lined up along the route. There was one person each to stain, to sandpaper, to fill, to spray, and each had to accomplish the task within fourteen minutes, after which a new unit arrived. The quality of the furniture was the best possible within its price range—good, substantial sets, liberally ornamented with carvings, produced by modern machinery mostly imported from the United States, with decent finish, good glazing and fair hardware. Mariage was, legitimately, proud of his factory, but he was forever searching for ways to do things better still. He liked the idea of carvings, but it bothered him that the machines failed to reproduce the sharpness of hand-carving. He showed me the blunted lines and hoped that by some miracle of coloring or finishing I would be able to make them *seem* sharper.

I had a room on the second floor of the factory, where I experimented and made my samples. The windows of my room overlooked the private garden of the Mariage family. One morning I was sitting near the window, reading, when I heard a cry for help below. The Mariage child, trying to climb a sharp picket fence, had slipped and was badly hurt. I ran down to help, but mother and child were already being attended, so I ran for my car and—don't ask me why—on the way I grabbed three or four carved chairbacks. Then I drove mother and child as fast as I could to the best hospital in Paris.

After dropping them off and calling Mariage, who was out of town at the time, I decided it was too late to drive back to the factory. Then I remembered the chairbacks. I dug them out of my car and took them to Rapseat, who ran over the carvings with his sandblast. The next morning, I drove back to the factory and put my sandblasted chairbacks through the line. The change was the miracle for which Mariage had hoped. It didn't make hand-carvings out of machine carvings, but to a great extent it made the ugly wormlike lines produced by the carving drills disappear. When the highlights and glaze were applied, only a professional could detect the difference.

By the end of my two weeks, I reduced the length of the finishing line by almost half. The 10,000 francs I received for this accomplishment saved Mariage ten times more every year. He, of his own will, doubled my fee for the idea of the sandblasting. Within a month it was part of the finishing process, and for a long time remained a mystery to the competition.

Making the Wood Old-Looking

Chapter Six

Elegant Fakes

The year was 1935; the place, my atelier in Paris; and the man who opened the door to my tiny office was Monsieur Sylvestre Baradoux, master cabinetmaker. Even though the late winter morning was cold and unfriendly, Baradoux was in his warmest mood—so much so that he agreed to buy a round at a nearby bistro.

Baradoux had every reason to be triumphant. An hour earlier he had met with an emissary from the Royal Court of Egypt and had received an order for most of the furnishings for a palace to be built in Alexandria. The order would keep Baradoux and his crew of forty craftsmen busy for at least two years.

My friend was blissfully ignorant of geography and had no idea where Egypt was, but as a craftsman he was a dogged and uncompromising perfectionist. After the third drink his smile faded, and I learned the real reason for his visit. It seemed that the Egyptian emissaries expected all the work to be of the first order, but in one room quality alone would not suffice: Only perfection would be tolerated—or else. The contract made this clear in rather frightening small print. The furnishings of the Blue Salon, thirty-four chairs and two consoles, had to be so close in design, shape, construction and finish to genuine Louis XIV antiques as to confound experts. Baradoux was to build new furniture with the facade of authentic 300-year old pieces—or else.

Now, my trade is wood finishing, and I am as much a perfectionist as my friend Baradoux. Said he: "You have repeatedly deceived me with pieces of furniture that I would have sworn were genuine antiques. I have been stunned to learn that they were younger than my beard. Now tell me, George, can we meet these stringent specifications, or shall I refuse the order?"

I had already consumed four aperitifs and in my elated condition I felt I could carry out the contract with my hands tied behind my back. I replied, "Sylvestre, my friend, you are crazy. You have received that once-in-a-lifetime commission, an order that every cabinetmaker in Paris would sell his soul to have. Yet you dare to think of giving it up? If we cannot carry it out, who can? Who? Take it, take it, take it." Thus began one of the most difficult tasks of our lives.

The layman is amazingly ignorant about antiques. Any crudely built piece of furniture, shaped more or less in the style of the period it represents, beaten with a chain, mauled with a screwdriver, dropped from the roof of the shop and repaired with sawdust and glue, will probably pass at auction. Compound these mutilations with wormholes made with an awl or with the legendary shotgun blast, and add a million flydroppings of dark shellac spritzed on with an old toothbrush through a bit of screening—such a piece would fool half of the experts. But the specifications of the Royal Court left no doubt that such a hackneyed approach would not do. They wanted perfection.

We began by ordering two truckloads of the best horse manure and by making sure we could obtain enough old wood, for using aged wood is the first requirement in copying antiques. Baradoux had a lot of old beams in his warehouse, salvaged from demolished houses. He also knew all the wreckers. Although World War I had been over for almost twenty years, the salvage industry still flourished. Timbers of choice woods older than 200 years were becoming scarce, but still there were plenty of excellent logs that had been removed from churches, ships, buildings and barns, all at least 100 years old and nicely weathered. Some even contained lively, hardworking worms in their bellies. The price was high, but so was the fee Baradoux was charging the Egyptians.

Using old wood in antique reproductions helps achieve the proper coloring, shading and finishing, but it also creates problems of strength. The function of a chair is to support sturdily and comfortably a person who may weigh more than 200 pounds. A new chair is

This is an original Louis XIV chair, much like the one Frank and Baradoux borrowed from the Louvre to copy for the Blue Salon.

built of sound, clear lumber that has been dried to a moisture content of seven to ten percent—wetter, and the wood will shrink, loosening the joints; drier, and the wood will be dangerously brittle.

Since the chairs would have upholstered seats and backs, we could use new, kiln-dried lumber for the hidden parts. The partly exposed parts, such as the back legs, were made of sound old lumber, but not too old. We cut the pieces roughly to shape and buried them for three months under a mound of horse manure. From the manure they picked up alkaline juices, the appropriate base coloring and the necessary moisture. The fully exposed parts, such as front legs and stretchers, got the same treatment, except they stayed in the manure only six weeks before being removed, cleaned, dried and shaped.

Our next problem was a basic one—we had to know precisely what it was we were copying. Fortunately, we both had done restoration work for the Louvre and other museums, and we could borrow a couple of chairs made during the reign of the "Sun King." We spent weeks studying these chairs, observing and noting every detail of their construction, carving, joining and finishing. We studied tools and working methods of the period, and once the wood was past the rough-cutting stage, no machine or power tool was ever used. Baradoux went so far as to confiscate from his men some hand tools he deemed too advanced.

I made him disconnect the electric grinders the craftsmen used to sharpen their tools. We replaced them with an ancient *meule*, a stone three feet in diameter that was turned with a foot pedal and revolved in a trough of water. Every man had to use this grinding stone, but no one except me was allowed to clean the water and the mud from the trough. I mysteriously saved this dirty water and mud.

Now, it is early summer, 1936. Baradoux and I sit in my shop admiring the thirty-four chairs and two consoles. We agree that they are masterpieces, but Baradoux wants to know: "How will you copy the 300-year-old finish of the models?"

My answer hit him like a bomb. "The finish of the model chairs is less than ten years old."

Baradoux became red in the face. Then he icily removed the covering sheet from one of the model chairs, pointed to the brass plaque of the Louvre and said, "George, you don't mean to tell me that this is a fake?"

"No," said I, "just that the finish is not old. I do not mean that it was refinished, but every time a servant polished it, waxed it or oiled it something was added to the original finish. So the original finish now is modified by 300 years of caretaking, carelessness, wear and accidents. These chairs were rewaxed very recently at the museum. Furthermore, I will have to copy all these nicks, caused by rough moving between the shops. Now you see, the finish of these chairs is as old as the last addition to it. To copy all of it I intend to use the same ingredients, the same ways and means that cause the models to look as they do."

I had done much research on the coloring and staining of the wood and discovered some surprising facts. One of the great achievements of Louis XIV was the establishment of the *manufacture des Gobelins*. It was not only a huge workshop where the famous tapestries were made, it was also a craft center where hundreds, maybe thousands, of skilled people found rewarding jobs. Joiners, carpenters and cabinet-makers worked not too far from the vats where the wool was dyed, and they soon discovered that most of those dyes worked well on wood, too. The art of wood dyeing progressed amazingly fast. Colorants were derived from insects, trees, weeds, fruits and minerals imported from faraway lands and prepared with lye, vinegar, soda ash or alcohol to produce all the colors of the rainbow.

Although the woodworker of the time would try out new colorants, in his own shop he usually stuck with the old proven methods of dyeing. The most important dye of the time was derived from the dried shell of the walnut. Brewed with some soda ash or a bit of lye and strained, this was and still is among the most popular and pleasant of dyes (page 22 tells how to make this *brou de noix*). Today, you can make this dye from walnut crystals or cassel extract. Dissolve the crystals in warm water. The more concentrated the solution, the darker the color will be. This dye will have more penetrating power if you add to it some commercial ammonia (about one pint to a gallon of dye), or some soda ash, also called washing soda or sal soda (about three ounces to a gallon of dye), or some lye (about a half teaspoon to a gallon of dye). Of the three, ammonia is the best for general use.

The wood most frequently used in the shops at that time was oak, and craftsmen knew that water from the grindstone would turn this wheat-colored wood gray or brownish gray, especially when the grindstone water contained some urine, as it often did. In theory this iron-rich water worked only on oak, but some smart carpenter discovered and used mordants, or prestains. The simplest of these was a brew of acorns, which conveyed the necessary amount of tannic acid to any wood. Then the grindstone water would work well on it also.

I had saved every drop of water from Baradoux's grindstone, hoping to use it to stain the chairs. But after three solid weeks of experimenting, the grindstone mud turned out to be useless. Finally, I hit upon a mordant mixture of equal amounts of dried sumac (a common American plant) leaves and acorn cups, brewed and strained. Washing down the chairs with this liquid imparted enough tannic acid to the wood so it would accept my final dye. This was the classical *brou de noix*, or walnut extract, described previously, modified by adding a generous portion of strong ammonia. The proportions of each component mattered less than the process itself—endless experimenting with the original ingredients to find the correct combination of mordant and dye, then refinement of the mixtures to obtain the perfect deep, brilliant color.

Personal observation is by far the most important factor in learning this, or any other, trade. Let me illustrate:

While working for the Louvre around 1930, I detected the faint smell of perfume inside a cabinet that had been made by one of the masters of the Louis XV era. I attributed this to accidental spilling and paid no special attention. A few weeks later, I came across the same sweet perfume inside another old chest. My curiosity aroused, I discovered the same scent inside many fine cabinets of the same period. Since perfume works by evaporation, it was hard to believe these interiors had been perfumed on purpose or that the smell could last through several centuries. My investigation drew a blank—no one could give me a clue about the mystery of the perfumed interiors.

In Paris every cabinetmaker makes his own *popote*, or polish, or has the secret of one. The *popote* is used to clean and restore the luster of old furniture. At the cost of many aperitifs I learned a number of these secret formulas, most of them childishly simple. Generally they consisted of rainwater to which a few drops of oil and alcohol were added, plus some Tripoli earth, which is a fine abrasive similar to rottenstone. Bolder craftsmen added a few drops of vitriol (a commercial version of sulfuric acid), to enhance the mystery of the product, not its efficiency. There was nothing earthshaking in any of this, until one of the old-timers disclosed that he dissolved some "benjamin" in the alcohol before adding it to the polish. This was new. I soon discovered that the proper name of the material was *gomme benjoin* (gum benzoin), and that it came in the form of pale rust-colored, peanut-shaped lumps. When crushed, it had the very smell I had detected in the antique cabinets. From then on, this subtle perfume became a trademark of my shop. In France I bought the benzoin in the paint store, but in America I had to order it from a large chemical company. The product I received was white, much like powdered milk, with no scent whatsoever. It had been refined out. To get the smell, one has to order unrefined gum benzoin, crush it and dissolve it in alcohol.

Observation, perseverance and a bit of luck also helped me find the proper luster for my antique reproductions. I observed that beeswax applied to the wood long ago had a dry shine, while freshly applied wax looked greasy. I had to reproduce the dry shine, and I decided that the way was to dissolve the wax in water, rather than turpentine or some other greasy solvent. I asked dozens of chemists, but the answer invariably was the same: Wax cannot be dissolved in water.

Still I never gave up. One day standing in line at the post office, I was able to help an embarrassed gentleman who had reached the window only to discover he had forgotten his money. A few hours later he was at my door with repayment, and we talked. He owned a small outfit that manufactured beauty products. He invited me to invest money in it, and his pitch went something like this: "There is money in cosmetics, the cost is negligible, the markup is great and so is the profit. The base of eighty percent of our products is wax in water. . . ." My heart stopped. Incredulous, I asked him to repeat what he had said: "The base of most of our products is emulsified wax." Here was the key—wax cannot be dissolved in water, but it can be emulsified in it. Not long after I had my own emulsion (page 115) and triumphantly, the dry shine.

This dry wax was the most important ingredient in the finishing of the furniture for the Blue Salon. With its help I could copy to perfection the shine and patina of true antiques. Moreover, I could easily mix dye into my water-wax to correct minor color deficiencies.

The remainder of the finishing secret involved some chain cloth from the armor of a medieval warrior, some old spurs, some shark-skin, bonesticks with rounded edges, and sunshine. The spurs reproduced spurmarks found on the models, very authentically. The old shops used sharkskin as sandpaper, and so did we. The chain cloth and bonesticks were used to burnish the waxed wood and to achieve silky smoothness. And nothing can replace the rays of the sun when you want colors to fade.

To the best of my knowledge, the Blue Salon is still one of the most beautiful rooms at the Royal Palace of Alexandria, but Sylvestre Baradoux, one of the fast-shrinking clan of proud and true craftsmen, died in 1961.

The Décapé

The English equivalent for the French word *décapant* is paint remover. The word *décapé* refers to an object from which the paint or finish is removed. To us wood finishers, the word *décapé* means a very special finish, and even an epoch in wood finishing. Let me explain.

During the 1920s, there was a feverish reconstruction going on in France. Banks opened up new branches, country houses were converted into manors, manors into chateaux and chateaux into palaces. During this boom in construction, many new ideas were initiated. One of these was to expose the natural wood hidden under layers of paint on paneling and furniture. As people realized that no painted wood could match the beauty of natural wood, this trend gained momentum. Early in the 1920s, Jansen started to cash in on this trend and hired Naveilhan.

By the mid-1920s, the *décapé* had become an accepted finish, and in 1928, Jansen exhibited in their show window the very first *armoire décapé*, a masterpiece of finishing by Naveilhan and me. During the next decade, the *décapé* was copied, imitated, bastardized and exported. One of its offspring, the horrible pickled finish, became quite popular in America. Only two outfits had the secret of the true *décapé*—Jansen/Naveilhan and George Frank. Never have I detailed the method of achieving this beautiful finish as I do in the following tale.

This Renaissance piece, part of Frank's exhibit at the 1936 Paris trade show, has a décapé finish, the basis of which is emulsified wax.

The Way to Mecca

The ex-Khedive of a certain North African country had money problems—he had so much that he did not know what to do. He cared for
his wife, their four children and his mistress in a manner befitting
royalty. As far as his needs or whims were concerned, his secretary,
Monsieur Boubli, saw to it that they were taken care of promptly.

The Khedive, a bon vivant, was a corpulent and jovial character,
well into his seventies in 1939, the time of this story. His latest flame
was the eighteen-year-old Yvonne. Court etiquette required that she
be hidden, unknown, discreetly kept. A short time later, the Khedive
purchased an estate about ninety miles south of Paris, complete with
a 200-year-old manor. Yvonne adapted quickly to her new role as
mistress of Ransonville and helped the Khedive spend money.

This being a true story, I have had to change the names of some
people and places. It is a fact, however, that my atelier at the time was
at 88 Rue de Charonne in Paris and that my office was a cubbyhole
with a desk, three chairs and a filing cabinet. From there I did not see
my two visitors alight from a Rolls Royce. One of them, who introduced himself as Monsieur Boubli, asked whether I would care to do
some wood finishing—removing old paint in a stairwell to expose the
natural wood. My affirmative answer was followed by a request for
samples. My two visitors then had a conference of which I could
understand not a single word, but eventually Boubli pointed to one
of the finishes and said, "This is the one His Highness would like you
to produce."

Soon after, my crew and I started the job at Ransonville. In less
than two months, the job was carried out to a beautiful conclusion.
The Khedive visited the work site frequently, and many nights we
shared a bottle of good wine with him. By the time I presented my
bill, I was no longer Monsieur Frank, I was "my friend, George."

"My friend, George," said the Khedive, "I am enchanted with your
work, but I have one favor to ask of you. I invited some friends here
for the month of Ramadan and they will be here in three weeks.
Would you please do the same kind of work on the six paneled rooms
of the manor?"

"Your Highness," answered I with a question, "to do the stairwell took us nearly two months. How can I do six times as much work in three weeks?"

"I'll help you," said the Khedive. "I can rub the wood as well as your men can." There was only one possible answer. "The job will be done," I said.

Before I describe the operations that followed, I must go back about three months, to when Boubli gave the contract to refinish the six paneled rooms to one of the leading interior decorators of Paris. He had about twenty men working on the job, not far from my four busy in the stairwell. There was a great deal of teasing going on all the time and some professional jealousy. My men even changed the labels on all our containers: The lime-water became angelmilk, the lye, laxative, and so on. The decorator's men finished first, almost a week ahead of us. The Khedive paid the well-padded bill without batting an eyelash and then asked me to redo the job.

The color of the wood in the stairwell was silvery gray, much like hemp rope, and the shine, or rather the gleam, of it was the dry shine that I developed using emulsified waxes. We left some of the old paint in the corners here and there, but except for that, all markings of the wood were readable and well emphasized. Not so with the panelings. Their color was a nondescript yellowish brown, with far too much old paint left in the corners. The shine was the greasy glow of fresh beeswax, with which the work was overloaded. The wood was fairly clean but it had no character. Yvonne expressed my sentiments exactly: "This is neither done nor to be done."

By the next morning the manor was alive with activity. Four more men arrived from my Paris shop with fishermen's hipboots, swim trunks and scores of brushes, half of them made of wire. Under my direction, some of the men started to take the paneling from the walls carefully, marking every piece for easy replacement. Others lowered the water level in the brand-new swimming pool to about two feet, and I dumped in about fifty pounds of caustic soda (sodium hydroxide). The paneling was lowered into the pool unceremoniously, where the potent solution of caustic soda and my hipbooted men wielding wire brushes made short work of the finish on the wood. The panels removed from the pool oozed ugly brown juices, the sap, coming from the guts of the wood.

Men in swim trunks handled the next operation, washing the wood until the water ran clear. More than once the Khedive and Yvonne joined the team. Helpers from the village wiped off the excess water and laid the panels on top of small brick piles, exposing the paneling to the sun (back first, face last). After drying, the panels were ready for the next step, the feeding with angelmilk—quicklime, freshly slaked in water. We painted this solution on the panels without much care, because after drying we brushed and wiped off all the lime we could. The fine dusting of lime remained in the wood, however, accentuating the silvery gray color the wood slowly acquired. We did not use a single piece of sandpaper, yet from the scrubbing and brushing the wood was pleasantly smooth and had the beginning of a glow.

The second day was not yet over when the first panels began their trek back to their original positions. On the eighth day, the swimming pool was drained, cleaned and restored by a caretaker. My men shed their hipboots, donned overalls and entered the manor, where the first room was ready for them. Their immediate task was to repair and to correct the damages caused by the work done so far. A number of splits had developed and we glued wedges in them, but not before rubbing their edges with strong tobacco juice or with "liquid nightmare," vinegar in which we had soaked all sorts of rusty iron objects. We did this to underline discreetly the fact that repairs had been made—we wanted the repairs to be visible. We used aged wood for wedges, and the fine brown or gray lines around them added credibility to the age of the repairs. My carpenters used as few nails as possible to reinstall the panels, hiding most of them under the crown molding, the base or the chair rail. The brads used to secure these were countersunk immediately and the holes filled with soft bread, moistened with saliva and tinted with powdered rottenstone. In two rooms we could not avoid using nails, so I devised a tricky way to camouflage them. The frames of these panelings were held together with mortise-and-tenon joints, pegged at each corner with two wooden pegs. No one ever noticed that when we finished the job there was a third peg at each corner, a fake that just covered the countersunk nail.

At this point the paneling had a silvery hemplike color, but the general harmony was missing. The wood had not been selected to be exposed, and some boards contrasted sharply with others. To lighten the dark ones, we used a saturated solution of oxalic acid dissolved in alcohol (kept away from any contact with metal). On some pieces we had to repeat this process two or three times. After bleaching all the pieces, we washed off the residue once with vinegar, and then a second time with ammonia water. Boards that were too light had to be dyed with various strengths of "liquid nightmare," which added to the anemic boards a grayish hue.

Painstakingly, we brought the colors in the room into harmony, if still quite far from uniformity, and began the actual finishing. After years of experimenting, I had learned how to emulsify wax in water and I could emulsify the two hardest waxes that exist, carnauba and candelilla. I made up vast supplies of this concoction, and we applied two thin coats of it to the panelings. After drying, we shined up the first coat with stiff scrub brushes. We rubbed or burnished the second coat with chain cloth. By now the wood was silky smooth, with fully emphasized markings and a natural shine. Yet the job was not done. My wax had another quality. In a few days it lost its luster and settled down to a low, matte texture. Now my stone wax entered the picture. Unrefined carnauba wax looks like green-gray rocks and is quite dull until it is rubbed, but then it acquires the most pleasant hard shine. I broke this wax into small pebbles, melted it over high heat in a double boiler and then, away from all fire hazards, I poured lacquer thinner over it. In a short time the wax gelled and became pastelike. With this wax, which dried to stone-hardness under my fingers, I coated the high points of the moldings, the carvings and other parts of the woodwork that were exposed to wear. A final buffing, this time with wool, helped us to achieve the finish that I consider the ultimate for this kind of work. The Khedive agreed and confirmed it in a letter that is still part of my treasured memorabilia.

The last day on the job was reserved for cleanup and for touch ups. With a tray in my hand filled with stains and brushes, I strolled from room to room and found and corrected faults nobody else could detect. One of the rooms was the Khedive's bedroom, furnished with austere simplicity: A huge bed, a few chairs and a single night table provided all he needed for his rest. I walked in the room, stepped on a screwdriver left there by some careless workman, lost my balance and fell. The tray slipped out of my hand and the contents of one of my small jars spilled on the carpet, which was of a quality royalty can afford, wood finishers never. I locked myself and my foreman, Richard, in the room and tried to clean up the spot. Two hours later we had to throw in the sponge. The spot remained. Then Richard had an idea: "Let's turn the bed around, and nobody will know the spot is under it." No sooner said than done.

The guests of the Khedive arrived the next day and the reception dinner was scheduled for 6:00 P.M. Well before that time I received a message that the Khedive wanted me to "honor the reception with my presence." Sensing that a simple wood finisher did not belong in the company of statesmen and political leaders, I tried to excuse myself, but Monsieur Boubli, the Khedive's secretary, made it clear that the Khedive would deeply resent my absence. Therefore, shortly after 5:00 P.M., I arrived at the manor in a hastily rented tuxedo. There I was promptly put at ease by Yvonne and the Khedive. A few aperitifs helped to narrow further the gap between diplomats and wood finisher, and by the time the couscous was served I no longer felt that I was an intruder.

After cognac and cigars, the Khedive took the guests on a tour of the manor. Politely he asked my permission to use his native language, and I guess that they spoke about the paintings, furniture and rugs, which represented a small fortune. When the group reached the first paneled room, I sensed that I was the one they were talking about. They looked at and stroked the wood, then looked at me with warmth. As new rooms opened up, the "oohs and ahs" of this appreciative audience increased. Finally, we entered the Khedive's bedroom. The bed was back in its original position, the spot was in full evidence, and my heart felt as if it had stopped beating. This time the Khedive spoke in French, addressing me directly, "George, my friend, under your magic fingers this lifeless wood has become a thing of beauty, like music or poetry. While performing your magic act, by accident you soiled my carpet. My intention is to keep that spot as it is, right where it is, to remind me of my indebtedness to you, who revealed to me the beauty that can be found in a piece of simple wood." Then the Khedive took me in his arms and kissed both of my cheeks. I had tears in my eyes and could not utter a single word. Then the Khedive spoke again, laughingly, "And remember, my friend, that a true believer can sleep only so that the line between his heart and his head points toward Mecca."

Questions on making the wood old-looking

I build Chippendale side-chair reproductions. My problem is finishing—I understand that the two most suitable finishes for antique furniture or antique reproductions are shellac and wax or hand-rubbed varnish. My chairs are made from Honduras mahogany, and I am wondering how to match the soft luster of the original chair while providing a protective coating. I am also concerned that I don't reveal a hairline at my glue joints, for which I use Elmer's Carpenter's Wood Glue.

Before finishing you must eliminate the hairline of glue. You can do that with warm water and an old toothbrush. Wipe and dry the wood, sandpaper it, and you are ready to stain and finish. The chair you are copying was probably made of Cuban mahogany, the best and densest species. It can be dyed with potassium dichromate (page 20)—a concentrated solution would turn the wood a deep, rusty red—or with quicklime-water (freshly slaked lime, strained), which would give a more purplish hue. These chemicals, however, do not work on lower-grade mahoganies unless the wood is prestained with mordants. The best mordant would be a brew made of the extract of logwood, although a brew of acorn shells may do the trick.

While the original was probably dyed by one of these methods, your best bet is to use water-soluble aniline dyes, which you can mix to the shade of your liking. Whichever method you use, I advise you not to try to obtain the final color or shade in one single dyeing operation. When I work on precious, fine pieces, I stain them sometimes five times with a weak solution rather than once with a strong one.

After dyeing the wood, the craftsman of yesteryear oiled it, and his favorite oil was made from linseed. When working mahogany, the craftsman soaked alkanet root in the oil, which gave it a pleasant red color. The root is not easily available today, but it can be replaced by oil-soluble aniline dye. Dissolve the dye in lacquer thinner and filter through a paper towel before coloring the oil with it. The tinted oil can also be your finishing material—it is up to you how many coats to apply.

When I use oil for finishing, I use boiled linseed oil, color it carefully with aniline dye and add to it about ten percent spar varnish (such as McCloskey's Spar Varnish) to hasten drying. I apply this very generously to the wood, leave it on for a full half hour, and then, with a rough burlap cloth, I take off as much as I can. Oil, if left on the wood, can become gooey, but when it is rubbed off, the remaining thin film acquires a pleasant luster. Do not be scared to use some grease with your oil: elbow grease.

When we restore antiques, the old brasses come to a beautiful patina with a little rubbing but lose that brightness after several weeks. What do manufacturers of brass hardware use to coat their brasses and hold that high luster?

Clear lacquer will protect brass and silver from oxidation and tarnishing. Most lacquer manufacturers have special lacquers for this purpose, so specify your need when ordering. Moreover, the metals to be protected must be absolutely clean before applying the lacquer.

I have just completed an early-American maple tavern table. The problem is the finish. I want to produce the worn, cracked patina of a table that has seen 200 years of use. I've experimented with some success but am not totally satisfied. Also, have you ever heard of using a smoke chamber for creating a patina?

If I had such a problem, my first step would be to get hold of a genuine antique piece to use as a sample. You may find such a piece in some nearby museum, and you may find out that the curator is "people," like you and me. Upon producing proper credentials, the curator may lend you the right object for a short period. My next step would then be to copy the model as closely as possible, but there are no set rules. One of my favorite methods was to look at my finish and, if it was not one-hundred percent satisfactory, to wash it off. Pitilessly, I washed off my finishes three, four, five times if I had to. Surprisingly, since each of these washings left traces and markings, they brought me always closer to the final look. You can use a smoke chamber if it helps you to get what you want. I have put items in chicken coops, in damp cellars and on sunny roofs and buried some in horse manure. Set your mind to it and your finish will look more genuine than the one on the piece you borrowed from the museum.

I am completing a copy of a Connecticut curly maple highboy. I have used fiddle back maple and would like to know what type of finish the original would probably have had and what would be recommended now? I would like to obtain a finish that will bring out the curl, but without the typical honey color seen on most maple.

The following cheap chemicals are probably available from your druggist: iron sulfate, copper sulfate and zinc sulfate. The iron sulfate is your best bet, since it will deepen the natural shadows in the wood, but watch the proportions, since it may darken the wood too much. Dissolve each of these chemicals in water, jotting down the proportions, and wet some samples. Also experiment with other primitive or home chemicals, such as urine, tea, coffee and vinegar, plus each of these with some rusty iron scrap soaked in it.

The person whose efforts you are trying to duplicate probably used one of these chemicals. The most important ingredient in wood finishing is experimenting. When you hit the stain or dye of your liking, the remainder of your problem will be finishing. There you have a limited choice: oil-varnish, wax or shellac. Since you are trying to imitate an old finish, modern finishes are simply out. Wax finish of bygone years is easy to duplicate. Use any good grade of paste wax, coat the wood with it and rub it clean. Highlight it with the proper color of shoe polish. But I doubt if I would like this finish for your highboy. The traditional way to a fine finish is French polishing (see page 60).

People and Problems

Chapter Seven

Having the opportunity to meet wonderful, exceptional people is the best thing that has ever happened to me. The next best thing is that sometimes, in some way, I am able to help them. A willingness to help people and actually helping them, however, are two quite different things. Let me illustrate with this sequence of correspondence with a carpenter's young helper. His first letter to me read: "I just graduated from high school, and before hiring me my boss asked, 'Have you got a toolbox? And tools?' I said I did. 'Have you got a sister?' I said yes, she is two years older. 'Then swipe one of her lipsticks, put it in the toolbox, and be on the job at 8 A.M.' I did that and have been on the job for four weeks now, but the lipstick is still unused. Was the man just making fun of me, or does lipstick really belong in a toolbox?"

I replied, "A lipstick is definitely a carpenter's tool, used to set locks or bolts properly. Rub some lipstick on the tongue of the lock and it will mark very accurately where the lock strikes the doorjamb. It will also locate obstructions properly and accurately when installing cabinets or paneling."

Later I received a second letter from the carpenter's helper. Here is the gist of it: "My boss was peeved when I told him your explanation about the lipstick. He dug deep in his toolchest and came up with a jar of yellow powder, labeled sulfur, and a hypodermic needle. Then he said, 'Ask that smart fellow Frank what these are for.' I'm asking."

I replied, "Veneer often does not adhere properly to the surface where it is applied. If this happens near the edges, you can lift up the veneer with a knife and introduce fresh glue. When this happens away from the edges, the solution is more involved. You have to make a slit where the veneer is loose and introduce the glue through that. However, the slit will be hard to disguise later. Therefore, smart old-timers prefer to use a hypodermic needle to inject glue into these problem areas.

Now, about the sulfur. It is one of the few elements that gains in volume as it cools off. If you had to anchor a steel rod, say, in a slab of concrete, the best way would be to drill a hole into the concrete, position the rod, then fill the gap with melted sulfur. As the heated sulfur cools off, it expands, anchoring the rod securely."

Do you think that was the end of the story? No. Another letter came, asking if I knew what sand was used for in a woodshop.

I replied, "I know of four different uses: 1) In the finishing room, where I always keep a bucket of it handy to extinguish fires (though I have never had a fire in any of my shops); 2) in the veneering room, where bags of heated sand are used to put pressure on shaped surfaces; 3) in inlay work, where, when the edge of a piece of veneer needs to be darkened, it is dipped into hot sand until charred; and 4) in sandblasting, to clean or decorate wood." For good measure I threw in the story about a wise guy in my shop. This fellow knew everything better than anybody else, until the day he found out that sand could be used by his co-workers in the dressing room, to fill up his shoes and the pockets of his clothing. That was the last I heard from the carpenter's helper. Do you think I helped him?

Some years ago I ran across a formula for making tack rags, but now that I am retired and working in my shop, I can't find it.

Rosin, or colophony, could be found in every old cabinet shop. We used to break it into powder (in a mortar) and dissolve a teaspoon of this powder in a cup of mineral spirits. We added a few drops of linseed oil and soaked our clean rags (linen is best) in the mixture, then squeezed out as much as possible. A less elaborate method is to soak the rag in mineral spirits and sprinkle a few drops of varnish onto it. With repeated squeezing you can work the ingredients together, then squeeze out all the liquid you can.

I buy clock movements and install them in cases that I make from western pine shelving. I finish them with a dark walnut oil stain and two or three coats of lowluster varnish. Lately, small round specks and short narrow streaks of pitch keep breaking through the varnish, sometimes within a day and sometimes several weeks later. I tried to seal in the pitch with shellac and with clear lacquer but I can't see any improvement.

This is an age-old problem and the easiest way to deal with it is to select a better grade of pine with less pitch. The second solution, which I learned in school but have never tried, is to wash down the pine before finishing with a fairly strong solution of lye, rinse with clear water, let dry and sand. The lye should remove most of the pitch, and it should increase the contrast between the hard and soft grain, making the pine more attractive. A third way, which I have done, is to set a match to the pitch and burn it out, then clean the hole and fill with tinted plaster or stick shellac. The difficulty is that you can do it only when a teardrop of pitch is visible on the wood.

I am building a French double harpsichord kit. The naturals on the keyboard have little slips of ebony glued on top. The instructions suggest dressing the ebony with urethane varnish thinned a little more than half with turpentine, to protect it from the oil of the hand. What do you think of a dressing of this kind?

On the sharps I have put slips of oil-free boiled beef bone because I have heard that over the years bone remains white while ivory will yellow. Is this true, and would the bone need a dressing like the ebony?

Finally, the instructions recommend putting two thin coats of 1½-pound cut shellac on the soundboard, to protect it without inhibiting its resonance. What do you think?

There are only two reasons to finish wood: to protect it and to enhance its beauty. If your harpsichord will be used by you or other serious musicians, the keys need no protection or improvement. Sandpaper them as smooth as you can and leave them alone. It would take fifty years for finger oil to stain them, so you can sand them again every fifty years. But if your harpsichord will be played by careless adults or children, you should protect the keys with two thin coats of polyurethane.

I believe bone can be bleached with hydrogen peroxide of 100 or 130 volume (your pharmacist can supply it). Before applying, soak the bone in caustic soda or lye, and wear rubber gloves.

The finish of your soundboard should be shellac. It's very important that it be fresh. Buy shellac flakes or buttons and dissolve in alcohol, and if you would really splurge, filter it through a paper towel.

Is there a clear, thin wood sealer (for dip coating) that will not raise the grain? I make wooden haircombs, and it is not practical to resand and repolish between the teeth. I have tried many finishes but I am not satisfied.

I would dip the combs either in a half-and-half mixture of clear lacquer and clear lacquer thinner, or into tung oil cut slightly with mineral spirits (about eighty percent tung to twenty percent mineral spirits). After thorough drying, I would rub in between the teeth with a nylon thread twisted into a strand, something like a horse's tail. Dip the horse tail in some fine garnet abrasive powder and hang it from the ceiling. Put a flat container underneath to recover the powder that comes loose. Then comb the horse tail until the comb is perfectly smooth between the teeth. With 4/0 steel wool I would make the outside as smooth as a good sales pitch, and my combs would be ready for market.

My father returned from Mexico with a beautifully carved quail in ironwood. I was admiring the finish, a fine semi-gloss with depth, and imagined oil being rubbed in with care. He told me, smiling, that it was shoe polish. Immediately I tried neutral shoe polish on a damaged marquetry piece, over Watco. It is beautiful. Something has to be wrong; it is all much too simple.

You can apply the best possible finish to roughly sanded wood and you will not be proud of the effect. On the other hand, you can apply shoe polish (which usually is composed of fine waxes) to a well-sanded piece and feel it is so beautiful that something must be wrong. No, fine finish nearly always can be equated with superior smoothness. Try to finish an unsanded piece with shoe polish and you will agree.

I have a coffee table made from a large slab of oak, bark and all. I sanded it smooth and applied Duroseal. It looks fine now except for near the center and one or two knots near the perimeter, which are dull and gray. Another coat of Duroseal makes the gray disappear, only to reappear when the finish has dried awhile. How do I seal in whatever that stuff is, without going to an on-the-surface finish, which would impair the natural good looks of the table?

I am almost certain that your problem is not one of finishing, and no finishing product will solve it. If I interpret your description correctly, you are trying to finish a piece of wood that is not properly dry as yet. The remedy is time. Let your wood breathe, let it get rid of all moisture, and your problems will be over.

I recently constructed a headboard of veneer plywood with solid cherry trim. The finish is Deft. The problem is the veneer seems to have soaked up more finish than the trim, resulting in a darker shade. How can I get a consistent hue?

If you use solid wood next to veneer made of the same wood, the veneered area will nearly always be darker. When veneer is made, the wood is submitted to intense heat and moisture. The fibers of the wood are broken, and they will absorb any coloring more readily than solid wood. I do not know any easy remedy. You could dye the solid parts with more concentrated dye or repeat the staining, until solid matches veneer.

I recently made a set of kitchen canisters for my wife. The materials are kiln-dried cherry wood, white glue and three coats of polyurethane inside and out. My wife is quite proud of them but she can't use them because of a strong odor inside the boxes. The odor is picked up by the flour and sugar and is detectable in items made with them even after cooking. I first suspected the finish so I removed it. That made no change so I tried covering it with two coats of lacquer. This made no difference, so now I suspect the odor is coming from the wood itself.

Healthy cherry has no offensive smell, nor has lacquer after it is dry. The smell in your canisters must have another source. For reasons unknown to me, animals, mainly dogs and cats, have a predilection to urinate on lumber. If cat's urine is the cause, you'll have a tough problem getting rid of the smell. Regardless, you must first completely dry the area from which the odor comes. Hang a low-watt incandescent bulb in each canister, and leave it on for a few days. Then wash the canisters out with a strong solution of ammonia water or Lysol. Dry them with the electric bulb again. If the smell persists, wait until a snow-clad winter evening. Light a fire in the fireplace. Ask your wife to sit on your lap, and burn your canisters. There will be no odor left.

Problems of smell occur frequently in vineyards, where empty barrels may have unpleasant odors. The accepted remedy is to light a stick of sulfur and let it burn out inside the barrel.

I am trying to reproduce the ochre-colored patina that maple and pine take on with age, but am having difficulty finding a chemical that will do the job. Can you suggest one?

To produce a faded ochre patina on pine or maple I would first carry out a few experiments. To start, make a strong brew of espresso coffee or chicory, strain it and apply it to the wood. This will create the base color. Assuming you intend to use a lacquer finish, add into your sealer and clear lacquer a bit each of white and French ochre tinting lacquers, checking continually to see how close you are to the desired color. This pigmented lacquer will produce a haze on the dyed wood that could be close to the effect you want. You could also experiment with a combination of dyes and pigmented stains. Use the coffee or chicory brew, and mix into it some powdered French ochre, some whiting and some glue. I would use hide glue, but rabbit-skin glue or even gum arabic or dextrine will do. The dye will produce the base color and the glue will produce the haze.

I have come across the term "ebonizing" in some books I've been reading on finishing. Sometimes it refers to attaining a grayish color, and sometimes to getting your wood totally black. What is the correct meaning of ebonizing, and what is the process involved?

Another of those ill-defined words is ebonizing. Ebony is a wood having the color of charcoal, so it follows that ebonizing should mean imitating this color (and eventually the matte shine of well-sanded ebony wood). Instead, many ebonizers try to create a totally black finish as glossy as they can make it. To my thinking, this is wrong.

Here is how I would ebonize my wood. First, sandpaper the wood as smooth as possible, wet it and sand again. Next, prestain the wood with a solution of logwood extract (page 23) or, if you can't find any, with one of tannic acid (about an ounce in a quart of water). After drying and light sanding, wet the wood with a solution of ferrous oxide (about $1\frac{3}{4}$ to $2\frac{1}{2}$ ounces to a quart of water), sponge the excess off and let dry.

This method should produce a deep, readable charcoal gray color, but if you are not satisfied, repeat the operation. Then spray on two coats of clear lacquer. After drying, rub out the finish with 4/0 steel wool.

Epilogue

The Water-Wax

Wax cannot be dissolved in water, but it can be emulsified in it. This fact, which I learned from a cosmetics manufacturer while working on the chairs for the palace at Alexandria (see page 98), led to the development of my water-wax. I guarded this formula throughout my life, but I will disclose it here.

Why the secrecy? Simply, business. The water-wax was the result of years of experimentation, the cost of which in time and money was staggering. With this wax I achieved finishes that the competition could not duplicate, and I had the guts to charge for them. I did not sell my water-wax cheap, but the majority of my customers were beyond the consideration of what was cheap and what was expensive. All paid the price, and none had the feeling they had been overcharged. In other words, this wax grew up in my hands to be a great moneymaker, and it was in my best interest to keep it a secret. Likewise, I did not broadcast that this wax, along with its many virtues, has shortcomings. The finish this wax imparts is beautiful, but fragile. It is like a silk dress—when you wear one, you cannot scrub floors.

In the early 1940s, I received a request to send a worker to a customer's home for some repairs. When I read the customer's name, Fritz Kreisler, the great violinist, I immediately decided to send myself. My wish to hear the great maestro playing while I quietly did my work was granted: Twenty feet away, Kreisler was playing his violin. But was he playing the *Tambourine Chinoise* or any of his other famous compositions? No, he was playing twelve notes over and over and over again. Three hours later I thought I was going crazy. I finished my work as quickly as I could and escaped from there.

What has this to do with water-wax? The great violinist sought something in those twelve notes that he could not find or master, as I sought, for many years, to find out how to impart to wood a hard, dry shine such as could be found on objects waxed centuries ago. I made up my mind that the key was dissolving wax in water, and this became an obsession. Although I wasn't too fond of beeswax and its soft, greasy glow, it was beeswax I tried to dissolve in water, needless to say, without success. Like Kreisler repeating his notes, I repeated my experiments over and over again.

One day, while holding a cake of unrefined carnauba wax in my hand, I sensed that here was part of the solution. I rubbed the wax and it smiled at me with the dry shine I had sought for years. I cannot describe the elated feeling I had, but the following weeks sobered me up quickly enough. I realized that my problem was not solved at all, that carnauba wax could be dissolved no better in water than beeswax. Only when the god of wood finishers made me meet the cosmetics manufacturer who innocently dropped the key word—emulsion—did I feel I was almost home. The emulsification of wax, however, was not so simple, and from professional chemists I had to learn the techniques. Hundreds of experiments later I arrived at the formula I give you now. It is the one I have used always.

In a nonmetallic container (enamel-coated is acceptable) heat a little over 3½ quarts of water (rainwater is best). When it boils, add to it a little over an ounce of triethanolamine, available from chemical supply houses. In another container, melt a little over four ounces each of carnauba and candelilla waxes—I prefer the unrefined versions of both, if available—plus about 6½ ounces of stearic acid. When this is melted, add slowly the wax mixture to the hot water. Let it cool, stirring frequently with a wooden stick. When cool, the waxes are emulsified and will have the consistency of heavy cream. The color will be a pale green-gray-beige.

As I have said, this is the best formula that I know. But am I satisfied with my water-wax? The answer is no. Without any doubt, through the use of my emulsified wax, I am far closer to the shine I am seeking, but I would be a liar if I said I was satisfied. The water-wax is far from being perfect. This is but one of the hundreds of wood-finishing problems that is open to research.

In closing, I would like to talk about three types of airplanes: The Wright Brothers', the Fokker of World War I and the Concorde. The first conquered the air and flew a few yards, the second flew well, and the third is flying faster than sound. This book is dedicated to Fernand Naveilhan, to whom I promised to do all I could to advance the trade of wood finishing. Naveilhan was to wood finishing what the Wright Brothers were to aviation. I am, perhaps, equivalent to the Red Baron, flying the Fokker. Who will fly the Concorde? I have done as much as I can, and I take my leave with this request. Take over, readers, and make out of the trade of wood finishing a skill, a science and an art.

Index